KINGDOM LIVING
Here and Now

John MacArthur, Jr. on the Beatitudes

MOODY PRESS
CHICAGO

DEDICATION

TO GRACE COMMUNITY CHURCH–
  MY BELOVED AND FAITHFUL FLOCK

© 1980 by
THE MOODY BIBLE INSTITUTE
OF CHICAGO

Unless otherwise indicated, all Scripture quotations in this book are from the
New American Standard Bible, © 1960, 1962, 1963, 1968, 1971, 1972, 1973,
1975, and 1977 by the Lockman Foundation, and are used by permission.

Library of Congress Catalog in Publication Data

MacArthur, John F.
    Kingdom living.

    Bibliography: p.
    1.   Beatitudes.   2.   Christian life—1960-
I.   Title.
BT382.M23   226'.9306   79-25326
ISBN 0-8024-4564-0

Printed in the United States of America

Contents

Preface

The Lord has recently impressed me with the need to preach the biblical doctrine of salvation. I have been deeply concerned that many revivalists, media preachers, and printed formula approaches to evangelism present an inadequate view of salvation. The church again is facing an age-old problem—the invasion of it by what has become known as "easy believism" or "cheap grace."

Many are jumping on (and back off) the Jesus "band wagon." People are told just to "believe in Jesus" and everything will be settled forever. Though touching on the wonderful simplicity of the gospel, such presentations are woefully inadequate when compared with the words of our own blessed Lord Jesus Christ in the Beatitudes.

Through an intense study of the gospel of Matthew, particularly the Sermon on the Mount, it has become abundantly clear to me what our Lord taught about the standards of true salvation. Specifically, the Beatitudes have hit me as never before in my life. They reveal the direction, if not the perfection, of the character of the truly saved, and they reveal the source of true happiness.

Of all the preaching series done in nearly eleven years' ministry at Grace Community Church, this one has brought a seemingly greater sense of conviction, more self-examination, commitment, and conversion of the lost than any other series.

The series is offered here, not so much as a book, but as it was preached—a series of messages from our Lord proclaiming the standard of true salvation.

I would like to thank Jerry Jenkins for his invaluable editorial help in preparing this book.

With the prayer that you will not be the same after hearing our Lord speak, I am gratefully His and yours,

John MacArthur

Anyone who runs ahead and does not continue in the teaching of Christ does not have God; whoever continues in the teaching has both the Father and the Son (2 John 9, NIV).

1
Examine Yourself

Jesus is in the happiness business.

Sadly, not everyone really understands or believes that. In fact, many Christians aren't sure they really experience true happiness. The very first sermon ever recorded as having been preached by Jesus Christ begins with the constantly ringing theme of happiness, and its revolutionary truth hit the world like a bomb exploding in the minds of those who heard it.

The truth of the Sermon on the Mount exploded in the minds of the original hearers because many of them were reluctant to have their standing before God evaluated by Jesus' strict standards. Such reluctance is present also among many professing Christians of our day. There is now an atmosphere of "easy believism" that allows people to experience an initial happiness in encountering the gospel, but not a deep, long-term joy derived from serious obedience to Christ's commands. Our Lord recognized the potential problem of an easy believism, as indicated in John 8:30-31, "As He spoke these things, many came to believe in Him. Jesus therefore was saying to those Jews who had believed Him, 'If you abide in My word, then you are truly disciples of Mine.' " Jesus affirms that an easy believism is inadequate.

The concept of easy believism is contrary also to the message of the New Testament epistles regarding salvation and assurance. The life of a true believer is never portrayed as a soft, do-as-you-please existence. The believer is called to a life of obedience, in which faith is verified by conduct. A life of obedience should flow from a Christian's basic relationship to Christ. The Lord's Supper illustrates the depth of a genuine attachment to Jesus Christ.

The Lord's Supper is the most wonderful, sacred, unique act of worship the blood-bought church of Jesus Christ can ever experience. It is a sacred memory of the cross and a time of self-examination.

The bread speaks of the body of Christ and the cup of His blood, and they point to the cross where He was crucified.

More than that, it is a communion with the living Christ. Jesus says in Luke 22:19, "Do this," so it is sacred as an act of obedience. I come to the Lord's Table as often as I can, take the most common things, and in my heart they become symbols of the body and blood of Jesus Christ.

Some Christians rarely or never come to the Lord's Table, just as there are some who are never obedient in baptism. Sometimes they are just ignorant; they do not understand the importance of the Lord's Table or of baptism. Sometimes Christians are just disobedient. They are acting carnally. But it may be that people who have no desire for testimony in baptism or fellowship at the Lord's Table are not Christians at all. They may *think* they are, but they are not.

Do you know what's worse than never coming to the Lord's Table? Coming to His Table when you do not deserve to be there. To do that is to eat and drink unworthily and be guilty of the body and blood of the Lord, according to 1 Corinthians 11:27. And verses 28-29 say, "But let a man examine himself, and so let him eat of the bread and drink of the cup. For he who eats and drinks eats and drinks judgment to himself, if he does not judge the body rightly."

It is a serious matter for a Christian to come to the Lord's Table when he has not repented of everything and does not desire righteousness and holiness above all. What is even more serious is to come to the Lord's Table and drink unworthily when you are not a Christian at all. Now do not quickly put this book down, telling me, yourself, and God that this does not apply to you because you have been a Christian for years. The Beatitudes call for a full self-examination. Such an approach Paul calls for in 2 Corinthians 13:5, "Test yourselves to see if you are in the faith." Prove it, he's saying. If it were easy to point to an experience in the past to prove your salvation, why would Paul ask you to examine yourself? There must be something else here.

You might be saying, "Well, *I'm* a Christian. *I* believe. *I* made a decision for Christ." A lot of people point to the past to verify their salvation, but did you know that the Bible never does that? It *never* points to the past. It always bases proof of real salvation on your life *now*. *Examine* (test in NASB) is a present tense continuous action, "Be constantly examining yourselves."

You say, "How do I examine myself and know if I'm really a Christian?" Look with me at Matthew 5. When Jesus arrived on the scene, the Jews had already decided what right living was all about. They had already built their own code, developed their own system of what it was to be holy. It was all external self-righteousness, and based on works.

Jesus shattered that when He said, "I want to give you a new standard for living, a new criteria by which you evaluate whether or not you're redeemed." He told them how a citizen of the kingdom really lives.

Do you want to prove yourself? Then let the Spirit of God compare your salvation to the facts of the Sermon on the Mount. Here is the standard, and the key to it all is one word: "righteousness." Jesus is saying, "If you are a child of

the King, the characteristic of your life will be righteousness."

Recently a woman told me of a lady in her church who
says she is a Christian, but who has been living with a man
who is not her husband. Is she a Christian? It is certainly a
fair question. First Corinthians 6 says that fornicators do not
inherit the kingdom of heaven. Why? Because fornication is
unrighteousness, and true conversion is characterized by
righteousness. Christians can commit fornication, but when
they do, they are not distinguishable from non-Christians.
So it is legitimate to question the woman's salvation.

The key verse to Christ's whole sermon is in Matthew 5:20
in which He says, "I say to you, that unless your righteousness surpasses that of the scribes and Pharisees, you shall
not enter the kingdom of heaven." They went to the Temple
everyday, they paid tithes, they fasted, they prayed. They
were religious freaks!

Yet Jesus says, "Unless your righteousness *surpasses* that,
you will not enter My kingdom." Righteousness is the issue.
Righteousness sets us apart as converted. Righteousness
simply means living right, living under God's standards, by
His definition. If we do not live this way, the genuineness of
our salvation is open to suspicion—to others and to ourselves (usually in the form of insecurity).

Hebrews 12:14 haunts me when I meet people who claim
to be Christians but whose lives do not agree: "Sanctification without which no one will see the Lord." Second
Timothy 2:19 says that the Lord knows them that are His.
And who are they? Those that name the name of Christ and
depart from iniquity.

Titus 1:16 says, "They profess to know God, but by their
deeds they deny Him, being detestable and disobedient,
and worthless for any good deeds." Profession means nothing without obedience, without righteousness, without holiness, without departing from iniquity.

Once, I actually heard a pastor preach, "Isn't it wonderful

that you can come to Jesus Christ and you don't have to change anything on the inside or the outside?" Can that be true? Of course not. There had better be transformation. Of course we can come to Jesus just as we are, but if we come away from conversion just as we were, how can we call it conversion? Second Corinthians 5:17 sums it up well: "Therefore if any man is in Christ, he is a new creature; the old things passed away; behold, new things have come."

Being righteous does not mean that we never sin. First John 1:9 says Christians are constantly confessing their sin. That certainly indicates that we do sin. But it is sin that we deal with sooner or later. We confess it, we turn from it, we repent of it, we despise it. We do not love it. "If any one loves the world, the love of the Father is not in him" (1 John 2:15). James puts it this way, "You adulteresses, do you not know that friendship with the world is hostility toward God? Therefore whoever wishes to be a friend of the world makes himself an enemy of God."

There will be a whole new approach to life. We will have sin, yes, but when sin appears we will hate it as Paul did in Romans 7. We will hunger and thirst for that which is right. We will seek to obey; we will seek to love our brother and hate the evil system of the world. That's the way it is, if true salvation exists.

You cannot prove that you are a Christian by waltzing down the same old path. Having made a decision, having walked an aisle, having gone into an inquiry room, or having read through a little book was never the biblical criterion for salvation. The biblical criterion for salvation is what your life is like right now. If it is not what it ought to be, either you are a Christian living in carnality, or you are not a Christian at all. Maybe only God and you really know which it is. Maybe only God really knows, because you might be deceived.

I say with an ache in my heart that I am sure there are many people who are not Christians in the very church that I pastor. As we shall learn from the next eleven chapters, if a person does not come to Jesus Christ shattered to the very depths of his being and mourning over his sinfulness, with a hunger and thirst after righteousness more than anything else, there is a possibility that that person is not a Christian.

Those are the criteria our Lord gives. He says there will first be a proper entrance into the kingdom. That is where He begins the Sermon on the Mount.

A lot of people come to Jesus because they think He would like to get in on what they have. We encourage that when we say, "Wouldn't it be great if big, famous so-and-so became a Christian? The Lord could really use. . ." God does not need that. What makes us think He needs someone's ability in addition to His power? No. If you do not come to Jesus on His terms, you do not come at all. His terms are brokenness, mourning, meekness, hungering and thirsting after righteousness.

Citizens of the kingdom are merciful, pure in heart, peacemakers, persecuted, reviled. You may have made a *decision* years ago that was not true salvation if it did not involve these things. Years later maybe you came back to the Lord broken over your sin. That's the moment it became real; that's the moment you entered the kingdom.

If you are truly a Christian, not only will your *entrance* into the kingdom be on this condition, but your *present testimony* will also be consistent with these virtues. In Matthew 5:13 Christ calls us the salt of the earth and in verse 14, the light of the world. If you are really a Christian, your testimony will be clearly, decisively distinguishable from the rest of the world.

You see, the world is like decaying meat, rotting. Salt is a preservative. That's why the Tribulation will be so horrible; when the church is gone, the salt is gone. We are the preserving agency in the midst of a decaying civilization. We are to be a light set on a hill, clearly distinguishable from the rest of the world.

What about our testimony? Is it evident to everybody around us that we are different? Or do we do what everybody else does? When we became Christians, did it change things about our lives?

Our Lord says that another thing that will characterize a child of the kingdom is obedience. We will long for the law of God (5:17-19). In fact, my sense of security is dependent on my commitment to obey. In disobedience I forfeit assurance.

Assurance is a gift of God, not enjoyed by a disobedient believer. Read what Peter says.

Now for this very reason also, applying all diligence, in your faith supply moral excellence, and in your moral excellence, knowledge; and in your knowledge, self-control, and in your self-control, perseverance, and in your perseverance, godliness; and in your godliness, brotherly kindness, and in your brotherly kindness, Christian love [2 Peter 1:5-7].

What is the purpose of such a virtuous life, such true spiritual character?

For if these qualities are yours and are increasing, they render you neither useless nor unfruitful in the true knowledge of our Lord Jesus Christ. For he who lacks these qualities is blind or short-sighted, having forgotten his purification from his former sins. Therefore, brethren, be all the more diligent to make certain about His calling and choosing you; for as long as you practice these things, you will never stumble [2 Peter 1:8-10].

The point is not that we are gaining salvation or even keeping salvation. Those great realities are bound up eternally with the sovereignty of God. Peter's point is that we may enjoy the sense of assurance, confidence, security that should accompany our entrance into the kingdom.

Neglect obedience and forfeit assurance. So, my salvation, my testimony, and my enjoyment of security are dependent on the reality of Beatitude character in my life.

In Romans 7 Paul longed to do the law of God, he

hungered to do the law of God, he delighted in the law of God, he loved the law of God, even though sin was always tugging at him. Are you really saved? Did you come in mourning over your sin, broken over your evil heart. Are you clearly distinguishable from the rest of the world? Are you obeying God? Is the great hunger of your heart to do that which is His will?

If you have really been converted, you will think differently. You will have a different heart. In Ezekiel 36:26 the Lord says that when someone becomes redeemed, He takes out the stony heart—the heart of obstinance—and puts in a heart of flesh, a new heart. Jesus told the Jews that hating and lusting were as bad as murdering and committing adultery, which indicates that the heart is the issue (Matthew 5:21-32).

When someone says that he is a Christian but continues in adultery, fornication, homosexuality, or the practice of some other sin like that, I look to 1 Corinthians 6, which says that those kinds of people do not inherit the kingdom of heaven. They did not come to Christ on His terms; they came on their own, and that does not make it.

Christ also said that if you are truly a child of the kingdom, you will have right words (Matthew 5:33). The mouth speaks out of the abundance of the heart. Jesus is saying that if your heart is set to hunger after righteousness, it will result in obedience. Obedience means you are thinking right, and when you open your mouth, right words will come out. Then when you act, right deeds will be the result. You will not retaliate; you will be kind. If somebody asks you for one, you will give him two. Verse 43 says that you will love your neighbor, and later you will love even your enemy. You will love even tax collectors!

In verse 48 Jesus says that the whole idea is to be like God. Don't claim to be a Christian because five years ago you walked an aisle. Don't claim to be a Christian because you once signed a card. Don't try to tell God you're a Christian because you went into a prayer room and talked to a counselor. And don't even tell yourself you're a Christian because some counselor told you that you were, because, at that moment, he didn't know positively, either.

Assurance is the Holy Spirit's work. He grants it by the inward testimony (Romans 8) and by the outer exhibit of works. Faith without works is dead, James says. Jesus puts it this way in John 8:31, "If you abide in My word, then you are truly disciples of Mine." He is saying you will be characterized by right thinking, obedience, right talking, and right doing.

Jesus also says a child of the kingdom will have right worship. When you worship God, it will be real (Matthew 6:1-18), not like the phonies who blow a trumpet, come pray, give, and fast to make a spectacle of their pietistic ways.

A true Christian will also have a right relationship with money and the world. He is not going to love money. Matthew 6:19 says that true kingdom people are not going to lay up for themselves treasures on earth. and say they are servants of God when their lives are bent on getting money. The two are incompatible. Trying to be both a friend of the world and a friend of God will prove to be impossible. If you love the world, the love of the Father is not in you.

In Matthew 6:25-34, Jesus says kingdom persons have a right relation to material things. They know God will take care of all that. Starting with verse 31, it says, "Do not be anxious then, saying, 'What shall we eat?' or 'What shall we drink' or 'With what shall we clothe ourselves?' For all these things the Gentiles eagerly seek."

The true child of the kingdom will have even a right relation to people. Chapter seven of Matthew says that he will not try to play pious when he has problems in his own life.

"Whew" you say? You come broken and contrite and shattered over your sinfulness. He changes you immediately and gives you a new heart, and you are different. You are salt, light, and on a hill. The world can see that you are distinct. Your life is characterized by a hunger for righteousness, which results in right thinking, right talking, right acting, right worship, and right relationships to money and things and the world. And you say, "Who could ever live like that?!"

Good, I am glad you got to that point. Because you cannot live like that. No one can. *It is impossible.* Jesus told the rich young ruler to sell everything he had, give the money to the poor, and then come and follow Him. But the rich man loved his money more than he loved Jesus, so he took his wealth and walked away. The Jews believed the rich could enter more easily into the kingdom of God because rich men could buy more sacrifices, pay more offerings, and give more to the poor. So Jesus uses the rich as the focus of His truth when He says, "Truly I say to you, it is hard for a rich man to enter the kingdom of heaven. And again I say to you, it is easier for a camel to go through the eye of a needle, than for a rich man to enter the kingdom of God" (Matthew 19:23-24).

Can a camel go through the eye of a needle? You say, "Well, He was referring to the Needle Gate." (Supposedly a small gate of those days that was troublesome for camels to pass through.) But He's not! He's saying exactly what He means: it is easier for a camel to go through the eye of a needle than for a rich man to be saved. "That's impossible." Exactly.

Verse 25 says, "When the disciples heard this, they were very astonished." If He had been talking about some Needle Gate, they would not have been so astonished. " 'Then who can be saved?' " the disciples asked.

Jesus looked at them and said to them, in effect, "I think you have the message. With men this is impossible. With God all things are possible."

Nobody, no time, could ever be saved by his own resources. Only with God is it possible. We do not have the resources on our own. We cannot do it. That is why we must be ready to cast ourselves on the mercy of God. The rich man wanted to climb on the religious bandwagon and bring his luggage of materialism with him, but he could not get on with such luggage. Instead of being a help, it was a curse.

The only way anybody ever enters the kingdom is when he realizes he can't, strips himself naked, and arrives back at Matthew 5:3 broken in spirit and mourning and hungering and thirsting for a righteousness he can never attain on his own.

Most people do not want to meet those conditions. They want to go to heaven their own way. They want to climb aboard with all their junk. They are going on a trip, usually with four bags: worldliness, sin, Satan, and self. They are saying, "Jesus I want the happiness You're going to give me. I want to stay out of hell. Here I come!" But they drop none of their bags.

There's a road for them, by the way. Go back to Matthew 7:13. The disciples, along with the multitude, were by this time probably saying to themselves, "With these kinds of standards, who ever qualifies?" Jesus says, "Enter by the narrow gate, for the gate is wide, and the way is broad that leads to destruction, and many are those who enter by it."

Why? You can go in there with all your baggage. It's a wide gate. Just take all the garbage you want. All your works, your self-righteousness, your I'll-do-it-my-way, and your I-want-Jesus-but-I-want-the-other-stuff-too approach. Verse 14 says that narrow is the gate and hard is the way that leads to life, and few there be that find it.

Have you ever tried to take four suitcases through a turnstile? You've got to drop all the baggage in order to pass. You've got to come in bare-handed. The broad way that leads to destruction is not marked "To Hell." On the contrary, it's deceitfully marked "To Heaven." Many are getting on *this* Jesus road. It's broad, and they don't have to leave anything behind. They don't have to live any differently or think any differently. They don't have to do anything! All they have to do is say, "I made a decision," or "I was baptized," or "I walked an aisle," or "I went forward," or "I signed a card," or "When I was a child, my mother helped me." The only thing is, such an approach is the wrong road. It leads to destruction. The saddest part is that *many* are on this road, and they don't realize it is the wrong road.

It isn't that decisions or baptisms are bad. They can be good. But often, only the routine of those acts is performed. There then is no genuine conversion of the heart. The same "many" on the broad road are those who will hear from Jesus, "I never knew you; depart from Me, you who practice lawlessness" (Matthew 7:23; see also 25:41).

Some have made "decisions" but have never cut the cord with the world. They have never given up their evil lifestyles. They still think that that decision or that experience will settle it. They are on the broad road and will someday arrive outside heaven and find, as John Bunyan says, that there is an entrance to hell from the portals of heaven. That way is easy, and there are a lot of people selling tickets to it.

Beware of false prophets. Matthew 7:21-23 says, "Not every one who says to Me, 'Lord, Lord,' will enter the kingdom of heaven; but he who does the will of My Father who is in heaven. Many will say to Me on that day, 'Lord, Lord, did we not prophesy in Your name, and in Your name cast out demons, and in Your name perform many miracles?' And then I will declare to them, 'I never knew you; depart from Me, you who practice lawlessness.' "

Don't lull yourself to sleep. Beloved, examine yourselves whether you are in the faith. Prove yourselves. These are God's conditions. Isaac Watts wrote:

> How helpless, guilty nature lies,
> Unconscious of its load,
> The heart unchanged can never rise
> To happiness and God.

> The will perverse, the passions blind
> In paths of ruin stray,
> Reason debased can never find
> The safe, the narrow way.
>
> Can ought beneath the power divine
> My stubborn will subdue?
> 'Tis Thine, Almighty Savior, Thine,
> To form my heart anew.
>
> Oh, change these wretched hearts of ours
> And give them life divine,
> Then shall our passions and our powers,
> Almighty Lord, be Thine.

To follow the broad road rather than the narrow is to be condemned, as illustrated in our Lord's picture of two religious houses. They both appeared to have the same structure, but their foundations were very different. One house stood, the other fell. Many on the broad road are building a religious house without Christ as the foundation rock. Their own works will prove to be sand. (See Matthew 7:24-27.)

Time may be short. How do you know? In John 12:32-34 this exchange took place, " 'And I, if I be lifted up from the earth, will draw all men to Myself.' But He was saying this to indicate the kind of death by which He was to die. The multitude therefore answered Him, 'We have heard out of the Law that the Christ is to remain forever; and how can You say, "The Son of Man must be lifted up"? Who is this Son of Man?' "

They had heard that the Messiah would live. "Jesus therefore said to them, 'For a little while longer the light is among you. Walk while you have the light, that darkness may not overtake you; he who walks in the darkness does not know where he goes. While you have the light, believe in the light, in order that you may become sons of light.' These things Jesus spoke, and He departed and hid Himself from them" (John 12:35-36).

What an illustration! He says you had better believe while you can believe. Then to illustrate that, He hid where they could not find Him, so that they might comprehend what it would mean not to have Him around.

In John 8 He spoke the same way at least three times. Start at verse 12: "Again therefore Jesus spoke to them, saying, 'I am the light of the world; he who follows Me shall not walk in the darkness, but shall have the light of life.' "

Then He said in verse 21, "I go away, and you shall seek Me, and shall die in your sin; where I am going, you cannot come." This is the second invitation, a warning that if people do not accept the light while the light is available, there will come a day when the light is not available.

In verse 24 He warned a third time, "I said therefore to you, that you shall die in your sins; for unless you believe that I am He, ye shall die in your sins."

Jesus was always extending His love, but also He was always telling them that there was a limit. There comes a time when God runs out of patience with sin (Genesis 6:3).

In Isaiah 63 we find this end of patience contrasted with the mercy of God in verses 7-10. The prophet Isaiah says in verse 7, "I shall make mention of the lovingkindnesses of the LORD, the praises of the LORD, according to all that the LORD has granted us, and the great goodness toward the house of Israel, which He granted them according to His compassion, and according to the multitude of His lovingkindnesses." What a verse! It talks about the loving mercy of God.

"For He said, 'Surely, they are My people, sons who will not deal falsely.' So He became their Savior" (verse 8). What a picture of God! He was so kind, so gracious.

"In all their affliction, He was afflicted, and the angel of His presence saved them; in His love and in His mercy He redeemed them; and He lifted them and carried them all the days of old" (verse 9). Oh, what a loving Savior!

But verse 10 comes like a lightning bolt to shatter the

peace of the scene: "But they rebelled and grieved His Holy Spirit; therefore, He turned Himself to become their enemy, He fought against them."

In the following chapters we shall look at the Beatitudes phrase by phrase. In some instances, many pages will be devoted to examining just one phrase. There is much practical and devotional truth that we can draw from these well-known verses, as many previous authors have done. But the main purpose for this book is not to be just another commentary on the Beatitudes. Rather, the book is a call for you to measure your life soberly and seriously against the standards of true righteousness set forth by the Beatitudes.

You might find yourself in essential conformity to the inner attitudes that Jesus outlines. In that case your assurance of salvation will be strengthened in a new way.

However, you might be surprised and caught short by the Beatitudes' strong words. You might be shocked. You might even be crushed in your spirit by lack of assurance. If this does happen to some of you, it is my sincere hope that you will let the Holy Spirit speak to your hearts and draw you to genuine happiness. Genuine happiness can come only when you know that Christ's standards of righteousness are the essential direction in which your life is pointed.

Many professed Christians are living in contradiction to their professions of faith. Some of these people are deceived and think they are saved when they are not. That is tragic. Their hearts and minds are hardened to the truth even though they have a "form of godliness." None of us should neglect such biblical warnings as Galatians 6:3-8.

> For if anyone thinks he is something when he is nothing, he deceives himself. But let each one examine his own work, and then he will have reason for boasting in regard to himself alone, and not in regard to another. For each one shall bear his own load. And let the one who is taught the word share all good things with him

who teaches. Do not be deceived. God is not mocked; for whatever a man sows, this he will also reap. For the one who sows to his own flesh shall from the flesh reap corruption, but the one who sows to the Spirit shall from the Spirit reap eternal life.

God is patient. God is kind, God is good, God is gracious, God is merciful, God is longsuffering, God is not willing that any should perish. But God's mercy has its limits. If you have not committed your life to Christ and come into the kingdom on His terms, you had better do it while you can. Come to the light while the light is available. Come to the Son while He shines.

2

"Happiness Is . . ."

Matthew 5:1-2

In the Beatitudes Jesus used the word *blessed* nine times. It simply means *happy* in the genuine sense of internal joy. We can read each reference to *blessed* that way. Let's begin with the entire text we will be covering in this book, Matthew 5:1-12:

And when He saw the multitudes, He went up on the mountain; and after He sat down, His disciples came to Him. And opening His mouth He began to teach them, saying, "Blessed are the poor in spirit, for theirs is the kingdom of heaven. Blessed are those who mourn, for they shall be comforted. Blessed are the gentle, for they shall inherit the earth. Blessed are those who hunger and thirst for righteousness, for they shall be satisfied. Blessed are the merciful, for they shall receive mercy. Blessed are the pure in heart, for they shall see God. Blessed are the peacemakers, for they shall be called sons of God. Blessed are those who have been persecuted for the sake of righteousness, for theirs is the kingdom of heaven. Blessed are you when men revile you, and persecute you, and say all kinds of evil against you falsely, on account of Me. Rejoice, and be glad, for your reward in heaven is great, for so they persecuted the prophets who were before you."

The ultimate point, in verse 12, is that these truths should result in rejoicing and exceeding gladness. But doesn't it seem paradoxical? Matthew's account presents a kingdom that does not really fit what most people would have anticipated. As you can see, happiness as outlined here in the words of Jesus is not exactly what you would expect.

It says that happy people are the poor in spirit, the mourners, the meek, the hungry and thirsty, the merciful, the pure in heart, the peacemakers, the persecuted, the reviled. You say, "Wait a minute! I'm not sure I want that kind of happiness! It sounds like misery with another name! You've got to be kidding!" But all the way down the line misery is connected to happiness.

There's no way around it. Misery is the key to happiness.

To most people, the whole thing seems absurd. One writer said it was as if "Jesus crept into the display window of life and changed all the price tags. It's all backward." Happiness comes out of misery?

The world says: "Happy is the go-getter, the guy who pushes everyone else out of his way, the guy who gets what he wants when he wants it, where he wants it, and how he wants it. Happiness is macho. Happiness is doing your own thing. Happiness is grabbing all the gusto you can get. Happiness is acquiring. Happy are the rich, happy are the noble, happy are the famous, and happy are the popular.

But that isn't it. The message from this King does not really fit the picture, and this is only the introduction to His sermon!

Like any good preacher, Jesus stated his objective at the beginning. The very start of the Sermon on the Mount tells us the whole point—that we should know real blessedness, real happiness, real joy, real gladness, genuine bliss, and divine reward. He goes on in chapters five, six, and seven to talk about what kind of life-style produces this kind of happiness.

Before we can understand this greatest single sermon ever preached, we must understand the foundation. We will cover the occasion, the preacher, the setting, the style, the recipients, and the teaching itself, but first we need to understand the context. I will be dealing with the biblical, the worldly, the political, and the religious contexts.

The biblical context

Where are we in the Bible when we come to Matthew 5? Just where are we in the flow of God's plan to reveal His truth to man? Well, we're at a new point, a place of dramatic change, a really incredible transformation.

Look at the very last message of the Old Testament, Malachi 4:6, where the Old Testament ends, "And he will restore the hearts of the fathers to their children, and the hearts of the children to their fathers, lest I come and smite the land with a curse."

Interesting. The Old Testament ends with a curse; the New Testament begins with a blessing. Now that's a dramatic change. The Old Testament: the Law, Sinai, thunder, lightning, judgment, cursing. The New Testament: Zion, grace, peace, blessing.

Our word *blessed* comes from the Greek *makarios*, an adjective that basically means *happy* or *blissful*. It comes from a root *makar*, which means to *be happy*, but not in the usual sense of happiness based on positive circumstances. Homer, for example, used the word to describe the Greek gods as being blessed in themselves, a state unaffected by the world of men, who were subject to poverty, weakness, and death. This is the New Testament meaning of *blessed*.

The Greeks called the island of Cyprus "the happy isle." They did this because they believed Cyprus was so beautiful, fertile, rich, and fulfilling that no man would ever have to go beyond its shores to find the perfect life. *Makarios*

describes that inner joy that is the fulfillment of every longing in the human heart.

William Barclay says, "Human happiness is something
that is dependent on the chances and changes of life, something which life may give and which life may also destroy.
The Christian blessedness is completely untouchable and
unassailable." (William Barclay, *The Gospel of Matthew*
[Philadelphia: Westminster] Vol. I, p. 84.)

Jesus said this happiness is the joy that no man can take
from you (John 16:22). It's an inner peace, an inner bliss, an
inner happiness, an inner joy not produced by circumstance. Let me take it a step further. *Blessed* is a word that
indicates character, touching man at the very base of his
existence. I say this because the word is used to describe
God. Many times in the Bible we find the statement,
"Blessed be God." (See Psalm 68:35; 72:18; 119:12; 1
Timothy 1:11.)

Whatever this state is, it is true of God. Whatever it means
to be blest and blessed, it is true of God and of Jesus Christ
(1 Timothy 6:15). Thus it stands to reason that the only
people who will ever experience it fully are those who partake of God and of Christ. There can be no biblical blessedness or happiness apart from that.

Peter tells us in 2 Peter 1:4 that we who believe in the Lord
Jesus Christ are "partakers of the divine nature." We can
know the same bliss, the same inner state of contentment,
the same happiness deep down within us, that is known by
God and the Lord Jesus Christ. What a marvelous thing!

Barclay concludes:

> The world can win its joys, and the world can equally
> well lose its joys. A change in fortune, a collapse in
> health, the failure of a plan, the disappointment of an
> ambition, even a change in the weather, can take away
> the fickle joy the world can give. But the Christian has
> the serene and untouchable joy which comes from walk-

ing forever in the company and in the presence of Jesus
Christ.

The greatness of the beatitudes is that they are not wist-
ful glimpses of some future beauty; they are not even
golden promises of some glory; they are triumphant
shouts of bliss for a permanent joy that nothing in the
world can ever take away. [pp. 84, 85.]

From the very beginning, then, the Sermon on the Mount
has nothing to offer someone who is apart from faith in
Jesus Christ. But for those who know and love the Lord
Jesus Christ, for those who by faith have become partakers
in the divine nature, the same bliss, the same contentment,
the same happiness, the same sense of *makarios* that is fun-
damentally an element of the character of God and Christ, is
ours. So, when we talk about happiness or blessedness, it is
from a biblical context and is not about a superficial attitude
based on circumstance.

Whereas the Old Covenant ends with a curse, the new one
begins with the potential of every believer's being indwelt
by the very character and nature of God. The Old Testament
is the book of Adam, and it's a sad story. The first king on
the earth was Adam, when God gave him dominion over it.
He was the first monarch, but he fell. Thus the Old Testament had to end with the threat of a curse.

But in the New Testament, there is a new King. Matthew
immediately presents the second Adam, the last Adam, the
greater-than-Adam. He is a King who does not fall to leave a
curse, but rather one who comes to reign and bring a blessing. The New Testament ends with a promise. (See Revelation 22:20.)

With the new King, a fantastic new reality dawns upon
human history. Here is One who can reverse the curse of
Adam. Matthew's gospel contains the ancestry of the King,
the prophetic anticipation of the King, the announcer of the
King (John the Baptist), the arrival of the King, the adoration

of the King, the advantage of the King in His victory over temptation, the affirmation of the King, and the activity of the King. Now we come to the address of the King: the manifesto of the Monarch Himself.

The Sermon on the Mount is the great statement of the King as He gives blessing instead of a curse to those who desire blessing. That's the general, biblical context in which this sermon was delivered. A new age, a new King, a new message.

The world's context

Jesus' message devastates worldly attitudes. You cannot fill a man's empty soul with external things. That's what the world tries to do. Jesus came to announce that the tree of happiness does not grow on the cursed earth. Yet so many seek it here.

Solomon was the most magnificent king who ever lived. If anybody should have been happy according to the world's standards, he should have been. He had nobility—his was the royal line of David through which the Messiah would come, the most royal, noble line in history. His palace was the paragon of the earth. And it was located in *the* city, the city of God, Jerusalem. His wealth was so immeasurable and his treasure so vast that the Old Testament says his silver was as common as rocks. His pleasure was fabulous food and incredible stables with thousands of the finest horses in the world. He had buildings, servants, vineyards, fishponds, and gardens. Women by the hundreds! And he was the wisest man who ever lived. He had it all.

By the world's standards he should have been an infinitely happy man. Yet all he had to say about it was, "Vanity of vanities! All is vanity." The word means *emptiness*. The New Testament teaches that man's life consists not in the abundance of things he possesses (Luke 12:15). If you're looking for happiness in the world's goods, you're looking in the wrong place. How ridiculous to think you can fill the void in your soul with the junk of the world.

Physical things do not touch the soul. It's a simple point, but think it through. You cannot fill a spiritual need with a physical substance. People try. If they're miserable in their marriage, they buy a new car or a new suit. That's foolish.

You cannot do the opposite either. When you're hungry, you don't want a lecture on grace; you want your dinner. And when you're dying of thirst you don't want to hear about the wonderful mercy of God; you want water. It's just as ridiculous to think that you can fill a spiritual need with a physical substance.

When King Saul was distressed, all the jewels in his crown could not comfort him. The book of Daniel tells us that King Belshazzar was carousing and drinking and living it up at a wild party like few in the history of any nation. Daniel 5:5 says that he was drinking wine in the golden vessels of the temple when a figure of a man's hand appeared on the wall and wrote that Belshazzar had been weighed in the balances and had been found wanting. The Bible says his countenance changed. The wine went sour and the food was like a rock in his stomach.

As the great Puritan saint Thomas Watson wrote, "Things of this world will no more keep out trouble of spirit than a piece of paper will stop a bullet. Worldly delights are winged. . ."(Thomas Watson, *The Beatitudes* [Edinburgh: Banner of Truth], p. 27). External things do more to discomfort the soul than to bless it (Ecclesiastes 5:13). When Jesus came into the world, he was not offering the world's stuff.

There are some today who pass themselves off as Christians and offer the world's stuff. They promise financial prosperity, success, popularity. Jesus never offered that. You will not find it in the Sermon on the Mount. Blessed are the poor, Luke puts it.

What God is saying in this marvelous, incomparable sermon, in these Beatitudes, is simply this: You will never find happiness in this world. Never. You might as well learn that. It is like seeking the living among the dead. You must ascend to another level.

The Sermon on the Mount will take you to that level. Are you ready? It's going to take you right away from this world and the things that are in it. It's going to counter everything you see on the TV. It's going to counter everything you hear by the fast-pitch salesman. It's going to counter everything you see on the billboards, everything you read in the magazines. It's going to give you an entirely different standard of life, totally opposite to what the world tells you.

You're going to have a tough time really living it if you do not learn it well, because it's going to be bombarded by everything that is represented by the world system.

The political context

The Jews were looking for a messiah, but their definition of a messiah was a political ruler. They wanted someone who would come riding into Jerusalem on a white horse and zap all the Romans in a revolution beyond anything the world had ever seen. They expected a real whirlwind deal when the Messiah arrived.

They tried to make Jesus a king in Galilee when He first began His ministry, John tells us, because they envisioned a welfare state. He fed thousands, so more showed up the next morning for a free breakfast. They thought this man was going to feed them, that He was going to bring constant welfare. The Jews may have been looking for a political kingdom, but Jesus never offered one. He told Pilate at His mockery of a trial, "My kingdom is not of this world" (John 18:36).

Jesus *never* brought up politics. He was not as concerned about changing the structure of society as He was about working on the inside of individuals. And this is what He says in His first sermon. The stress is on being. It's not on ruling or possessing. He's not after what men do; He's after what men are, because what they are will determine what they do.

The ideals in the Sermon on the Mount are contrary to human ideas about government and kingdoms. In fact, the most exalted people in Christ's kingdom would be the lowest of the low in the world's eyes. Do you know who was the greatest man who ever lived up to that time? As far as the world was concerned he was nothing but an eccentric religious fanatic who lived in the wilderness. He was not even part of the religious system, yet Jesus said John the Baptist was the greatest man who ever lived. (See Matthew 11:11.)

Then He went on to say, in effect, "But there's one greater than he. You know who it is? The least in My kingdom." The poor in spirit, the mourning, the meek, those who hunger and thirst, feel empty inside, those full of mercy, those pure in heart, those who make peace, those who are persecuted, those who are reviled, those who have all manner of evil spoken against them falsely.

Doesn't that sound like the biggest bunch of losers you've ever heard of? By the world's standards, they are. The world says exert yourself, demand your rights, be a big shot, push yourself up, hold onto your pride. But Christ has a different kind of kingdom. It even advocates the acceptance of persecution without retaliation, and it blesses those who live that way. So the political aspect of this message was devastating. It was the opposite of what the Jews expected a Messiah to say, and compared to what they anticipated, Christ was not political at all.

The religious context

Jesus was confronting a whole society of religionists, professional ritualists. There were four main groups within the religion of Judaism: Pharisees, Sadducees, Essenes, and Zealots. Let me suggest some simple, general insights into each group.

The Pharisees believed happiness was found in tradition

or legalism. They were hot on the past. To them, real happiness came through obeying the traditions of the fathers.

The Sadducees believed happiness was found in the present, in modernism and liberalism. We're here, they would say; we've got to interpret things according to modern standards. Theirs was an updated religion, a brand new liberalism. Chuck the old stuff.

(In a sense, both the Pharisees and the Sadducees had a little, tiny bit of truth. True religion has to be based on the past. And true religion has to work in the present.)

Then there were the Essenes who said, "No, happiness is in separation from the world." Ooh, that sounds good, doesn't it? Only they were stressing geographical separation. They just moved out of town.

Then there were the Zealots who said happiness was found in political revolution, in knocking off Rome.

So, the Pharisees were saying go back. The Sadducees were saying go ahead. The Essenes were saying go out. And the Zealots were saying go against.

The Pharisees were nostalgia buffs. The Sadducees were modernists. The Essenes were isolationists. And the Zealots were social activists. What a mess! Sounds just like today!

Jesus' point was: you're all wrong. Every one of you. For the Pharisees He was saying religion is not external observance. To the Sadducees He was saying, "Religion is not human philosophy invented to accommodate the new day." To the Essenes He was saying, "Believe Me, religion is not geographic separation." And to the Zealots He was saying, "Neither is religion social activism."

What He *was* saying is this: "My kingdom is inside." That's the whole point, the message of Jesus to the world. That's the whole basis of the Sermon on the Mount. It's inside, not outside. Not ritual, not philosophy, not location, not activism. Jesus here is cracking open the door on the New Covenant, of which Jeremiah had said that God would write His law on their *inward* parts (Jeremiah 31:33).

Jesus summed it up, "Unless your righteousness surpasses that of the scribes and Pharisees, you shall not enter the kingdom of heaven" (Matthew 5:20). In other words, unless you've got more going for yourselves than that external stuff, you've got no part in My kingdom.

The same is true today. We cannot comfort ourselves because we are sitting on the right traditional view of theology. The liberals cannot comfort themselves because they have spun off some great new (really very old) theory that the Bible is not the Word of God.

A man cannot comfort himself in the fact that he has moved into some monastery where he sits and contemplates God, undistracted by the things of the world. Nor can a man comfort himself merely because he calls himself a social activist and runs all over the place trying to straighten out social problems.

Those are not the things Jesus is after. Ultimately all those things have a part of the truth, don't they? We need to be socially involved and we need to be set apart unto God. And we need to be contemporary and we need to be based on the past, but in and of themselves, these things are external. God is after what is on the inside.

Way back in 1 Samuel 16:7 God laid it out when He said, "The LORD looks at the heart." Proverbs 4:23 says, "Watch over your heart . . . for from it flow the springs of life." You'd better guard your heart. That's the issue. If we took care of our spiritual hearts the way we take care of our physical hearts, it would be amazing, wouldn't it? People are going crazy over protecting their hearts. There are joggers everywhere. People riding bicycles. Up and down hills. Got to take care of that heart!

When the Bible says you'd better guard the heart, it's talking about your spiritual self. In the Hebrew, it includes the seat of all your knowledge of God. The Williams translation expresses well what Jesus said in Luke 11:39-41, "Now you Pharisees have the habit of cleaning the outside of your cups and dishes, but inside you yourselves are full of greed and wickedness. You fools! Did not the One who made the outside make the inside too? But dedicate once for all your inner self, and at once you will have everything clean.''

On the basis of that overview of those contexts, there are at least five reasons that it is important to study the Sermon on the Mount:

1. Because it shows the necessity of the new birth. We can never please God on our own, in our flesh. The only people who will know blessedness are the people who are partakers of the divine nature of God. The Sermon on the Mount strengthens the Law of Moses in showing us the need for salvation. In the Law of Moses you hear about not doing this and not doing that—the emphasis is dealing with actions. The Sermon on the Mount gets down more directly to attitudes. It says you cannot live one day in a blest condition apart from the new birth in Jesus Christ. It shows the desperate situation man is in without God.

2. It clearly points to Jesus Christ and is perhaps the single greatest insight into His mind. Do you want to know how He thinks? Study His sermon. Do you want to know where His heart really beats? Study His sermon. Do you want to know what He really feels about living and about life? Study His sermon.

3. It's the only way to happiness for Christians. If you want to be happy, if you want to be filled with the Spirit, don't go seeking some mystical experience. Don't chase some elusive dream. Don't pop from one meeting to another trying to catch it in the air. Just master the Sermon and put it into practice.

4. It's the best means of evangelism I know. Surprised? If we ever really live out the Sermon on the Mount, we'll knock the world over for Christ.

5. It pleases God. That's a privilege. That sinful people, like

you and me, could please God. What an incredible thought!

So, there is plenty of reason to study the Sermon on the Mount, to give ourselves to it. Let's look closely then at the first two verses.

Verse 1 begins, "And when He saw the multitudes." Jesus was always moved by the multitudes, and he cared for them. Matthew 9:36, 14:14, and 15:32 record that when He saw the multitudes, He had compassion.

This particular multitude is described in verses 23-25 of chapter four, in which it tells of Jesus' having gone all about Galilee, teaching in the synagogues, preaching the gospel of His kingdom, healing the sick. His fame had spread in every direction and "great multitudes followed Him from Galilee and Decapolis and Jerusalem and Judea and from beyond the Jordan."

Here was this mass of humanity coming from north, south, east, and west, and when He saw them, as always, His heart was broken. When He saw them hungry, He gave them food. When He saw the spiritual hunger of their hearts, He reached out to give them what their spirits needed.

Crowds surged after Christ. All sorts of people. Sick, demon-possessed, Pharisees, Sadducees, Essenes, Zealots, ritualists, harlots, publicans, scholars, illiterates, refined, degraded, rich men, beggars. There was some strange attractiveness in Christ that knew nothing of class or rank.

His message really was first to the disciples, not to the multitude, but He wanted the multitude to hear it. They couldn't live it out. They couldn't know this blessedness. But they could at least know it was available. They were the secondary audience, but they were what prompted the message.

He went up into a mountain. He was seated. His disciples came to Him and He opened His mouth and taught them.

Who is this Preacher of whom they said, "Never did a man speak the way this man speaks" (John 7:46)? Of whom it was said, "He was teaching them as one having authority, and not as the scribes" (Mark 1:22). He didn't quote any sources. He spoke with an authority all His own. What a Preacher!

His sermon is a great illustration of homiletics. It has three points (You can't get any better homiletics than that!): the citizens of the kingdom, the righteousness of the kingdom, and the exhortation to enter the kingdom. Then, in the last part of chapter seven, we see the effect of the sermon. It's homiletic. It flows beautifully from one thing to another with magnificent transitions.

The master Preacher had structure, He had power, He had a divine commission. To one of the Old Testament prophets God had said, "I will make your tongue stick to the roof of your mouth so that you will be dumb, and cannot be a man who rebukes them" (Ezekiel 3:26). But later God came to the same prophet and allowed him to say, "Now the hand of the Lord had been upon me in the evening. . . . so my mouth was opened, and I was no longer speechless. Then the word of the LORD came to me" (Ezekiel 33:22).

Our Lord Jesus Christ, with all the power and intellect only God could have, developed a sermon like no other sermon, yet restricted His mouth until God's sovereign will and timing opened it.

Look at verse 1 again. He went into a mountain. The Greek adds *the* mountain. What mountain? No mountain in particular. (It had no name.) It's just a hill that slopes down the north shore of the Sea of Galilee right to the lovely, green, sunlit water—one of the most magnificent scenes anywhere. It is surrounded by the gentle hills of Galilee on the right and the Golan Heights on the left, and a few miles down, the beginning of the Jordan River, descending down the Jordan Valley to the Dead Sea.

To the right and over the hills to the west is the Valley of

Sharon, and then the Mediterranean. There on that little hill, Jesus sat and spoke. It wasn't anything but *a* mountain, so why does the Greek say *the* mountain? It wasn't *the* mountain until He gave His sermon. It was *the* mountain when Matthew wrote it because Jesus had a way of sanctifying the very place.

He was seated. He opened His mouth. He taught them. He sat because that was the traditional way a rabbi taught. When he sat and spoke, that was official. That's true even today. When a professor is given an assignment at a university, we say he is given "the chair." The Roman Catholic Church tells us that the Pope speaks ex cathedra, "from his chair."

What Jesus was saying was not some random thought; it was the official manifesto of the King. "And opening His mouth" is a colloquialism in Greek. It is used to describe solemn, grave, dignified, serious, weighty statements. This phrase is also used in some extra-biblical references to speak of someone who is sharing intimately from his heart.

"His disciples came to Him." They were the primary targets because they were the only ones who could know the blessedness of which He spoke. They were the only ones who could live the Sermon on the Mount because they were the only partakers of God's own power and presence in their lives.

That's possible for us only as we know Jesus Christ. The late Archbishop McGee of England reportedly said once that it was impossible to conduct the affairs of the English nation on the basis of the Sermon on the Mount because the nation was not loyal to the King. No one can live the Sermon on the Mount unless he knows the King. The disciples knew Him, so they were the primary audience. To the rest, it was an invitation to know Him.

The lesson itself comes in verses 3-12. Blessed, blessed, blessed, blessed. Oh, it's a tremendous teaching. What He says here is so profound, so life changing, as we will see.

You can't study the Sermon on the Mount and be the same. I can't. The truths we shall consider in the Beatitudes are deep and demanding, and are not for the half-hearted. Let's commit ourselves to be the kind of people God wants us to be, remembering that we have the capacity, if we know the Lord Jesus Christ, to appropriate kingdom living into our lives.

3

"Happy Are the Nobodies . . ."

Matthew 5:3

"Blessed are the poor in spirit, for theirs is the kingdom of heaven." Don't be dismayed that this entire chapter is devoted to just one verse. Some verses are so loaded with exciting truth that they deserve a chapter's worth of commentary.

A good tongue-in-cheek illustration of pride, which sin God hates, was provided recently by the noted radio pastor, C. Donald Cole of the Moody Bible Institute when he prefaced some remarks with this statement: "For the next few moments I'm going to say some truly remarkable things about pride."

Of course, the truly proud person rarely sees himself as such, for if he did, he would readily see that his life-style is antithetical to Jesus' new message in the introduction to the Sermon on the Mount. He is offering blessing and happiness based on a new kind of living, a righteous ideal, a selfless standard. This greatest sermon ever preached focuses on just that kind of happiness—that which comes to the selfless.

I believe this message is for all of us. Historically some

evangelicals have objected to the Sermon on the Mount on the grounds that it is too hard. For instance, when Christ says in Matthew 5:48, "You are to be perfect, as your heavenly Father is perfect," they say that that's too hard and pass it off to the Millennium. They say the sermon must be principles for the kingdom life. But frankly, there are many problems with that view.

First, the text does not say this is for the Millennium. Second, Jesus preached it to people who were not living in the Millennium. (That seems to be the strongest argument of all.) Third, it becomes confusing if you push it into the Millennium because it says you are blessed when you are persecuted for righteousness's sake and when men revile you and persecute you and say evil things against you falsely. Who is going to get away with that in the kingdom?

Matthew 5:44, "love your enemies, and pray for those who persecute you," would become meaningless. Anyway, as we shall see, every principle in the Sermon on the Mount is also found somewhere else in the New Testament. We cannot relegate the whole thing to some super saints in the future form of the kingdom.

This is for us. It is the distinctive life-style of a believer of any age. It calls upon us to come to a new standard of living. Jesus is saying, "Look, this is the way you must live if you are to know happiness." Isn't it wonderful that God is not a cosmic killjoy, as the world would like us to believe? That He is not intent upon raining on your parade? God wants us to be happy. God wants us to be blessed. And He gives us the principles by which we can be.

This is distinctive living. Live like this and I promise that you will be different. There are not many people living out the sermon, and even many Christians today seem to have lost the distinctiveness that the sermon principles give to life. We have been shaped by the world, squeezed into its mold in terms of music, morals, marriages, divorces, liberation movements, materialism, diet, alcohol, dance, sports, business ethics, dress, entertainment, and all kinds of things. But God wants us to live differently. He says if you live this way, you will be happy. And it begins with poverty of spirit.

When I buy a car, the first thing I do is read that little book that comes with it that tells me how to operate and maintain it. I know the basics, but there is much I need to know and I figure the manufacturer who wrote the book knows the product far better than anyone else I could consult. The manufacturer of everybody in the world is God, yet very few people turn to Him to find out how to run their lives. They should be asking God how they can know fulfillment. "You made me, You tell me." And Jesus does. Right here.

He's dealing with the inside. That doesn't mean there's no commitment to the outside. But when the inside is right, the outside is right. Faith without works is dead. You are created in Christ Jesus unto good works. But the real outside can be produced only by the real inside. If that sounds like a bit of a paradox, you'll notice that all the Beatitudes are like sacred paradoxes—they are given in contrast to everything the world thinks.

The word *blessing* or *blessed*, which we have defined as happiness or bliss from the Greek *makarios*, has an opposite in Scripture. It is *ouie* and we translate it *woe*. Jesus does not say, "I wish you blessedness." He says, "Blessed is the man who." And when He in contrast says, "Woe to the man who," He is not simply wishing; He is, in both cases, making judgmental pronouncements.

Look at the sequence of these pronouncements in the Beatitudes. We see first the poor in spirit, which is the right attitude toward sin and which leads to mourning in verse 4. After you've seen your sinfulness and mourned, you're meek with a sense of humility. Then you seek and hunger and thirst for righteousness. Do you see the progression? That manifests itself in mercy (v. 7), in purity of heart (v. 8), in a peacemaking spirit (v. 9). The result of being merciful and pure in heart and peacemaking is that you are reviled and persecuted and falsely accused. Why? Because by the time you have been poor in spirit and mourned over it, become humble, sought righteousness, lived a merciful, pure, and peacemaking life, you have sufficiently irritated the world.

But when it's all said and done, verse 12 says you can rejoice and be exceeding glad, for great is your reward in heaven. And when you live like that, you can be sure that verse 13 is true: you are the salt of the earth. That's what it takes. You are the light of the world. You can't be salt and light, you can't get to verse 13 unless you start at verse 3. So let's look at verse 3.

Why does Christ begin with the poor in spirit? He's talking about a new kind of living, a new standard, a new way to live, so why begin here? What makes this the source of happiness? Well, because it is the fundamental characteristic of a Christian. Becoming poor in spirit is the very first thing that must happen in the life of anybody who ever enters God's kingdom. Nobody ever entered on the basis of pride. The doorway is very low, and only people who crawl can come in.

Paradoxically, we know there is a mountain to climb, heights to scale, a standard to attain, but sooner or later we realize we are incapable of attaining it. The sooner we realize it, the sooner we are on our way to finding the One who will attain it for us. In other words, Jesus is saying, "You can't be filled until you're empty. You can't be worthwhile until you're worthless."

It amazes me that in modern Christianity there is so little of the self-emptying concept. I've seen a lot of books on how to be filled with joy and filled with the Spirit and filled with this and filled with that, but how about a book on how to empty yourself of self? Can you imagine a book entitled, *How to Be Nothing?* Or, *How to Be a Nobody?* Real bestsellers, don't you think?

Poverty of spirit is the foundation of all graces, yet so much of our modern Christianity feeds on pride. You might as well expect fruit to grow without trees if you think the graces of the Christian life grow without humility. As long as we are not poor in spirit, we cannot receive grace. You can't even become a Christian unless you're poor in spirit. As you live your Christian life, then, you will never know the other graces as long as you violate poverty of spirit.

Jesus is saying, "Start here; happiness is for the humble." Until we are humble, Christ is never precious to us. We can't see Him for looking at ourselves instead. Because we see our own wants and our own needs and our own desperation, we never see the matchless worth of Christ. Until we know how damned we are, we cannot appreciate how glorious He is. Until we see our poverty, we cannot understand His riches. Out of the carcass comes the honey. In our deadness we come alive. No man ever comes to Jesus Christ and enters the kingdom without crawling, without a terrible sense of sinfulness and repentance. Proverbs 16:5 says that the proud are an abomination.

God gives grace to the humble. That's why this has to be at the very beginning. The only way to come to God is to confess unrighteousness, confess inability to meet God's standards, confess that you can't do it. You enter with a sense of helplessness and desperation to receive divine blessing, and you maintain that sense in order to know continual happiness as you live in Christ. It sounds paradoxical, but it works, as we will see.

How many fools there are in the world who never see the truth. Even Christians who came to God with the right attitude have been swept into modern Christianity's exaltation of the individual. In our flesh we have nothing. That's why Christ began his sermon where He did.

What exactly does it mean to be "poor in spirit"? What kind of poverty is he talking about?

Some suggest that it's a material poverty. But if Christ

means just the people without money, then the worst thing we can do as Christians is to give someone money! Assisting the poor would be terrible. Feeding the hungry would be ridiculous. We would have to stop any aid to the needy. In fact, what we really would have to do is just get all the money out of everybody we can so they will all be poor and qualify for God's kingdom. Then we'd be good missionaries, right? Trouble is, then we would have money and we would be left out!

God is not talking about material poverty. In fact, David said he never saw the righteous forsaken or his seed begging bread (Psalm 37:25). Though the apostle Paul had times of hunger and thirst, he was never a beggar. The Lord Jesus never went around begging for food. He and His disciples were accused of being mad, and they were accused of being ignorant, and they were accused of turning the world upside down, but they were never accused of being beggars. (If they had been, surely the Pharisees would have added that to their accusations.)

So, what kind of poverty is this? Christ tells us: poor in spirit, poverty of spirit. The word *poor* is from the Greek *ptokas,* a noun that means poor in this world's goods; a beggar, desperately ashamed even to allow his identity to be known. It is not just poor, it is begging poor. (There is another word in the Bible for normal poverty, *penace,* which means you are so poor that you have to work just to maintain your living.) *Ptokas* means you're so poor you have to beg. *Penace,* you can earn your own living. *Ptokas,* you have no resource in yourself even to live. You're totally dependent on somebody else.

"Now that," says Jesus, "is a happy man."

What? Again it sounds absurd, doesn't it? Well, we've already established that He's not talking about physical poverty. He's talking about poverty of spirit and using the word that best compares with destitute need. This is the best analogy to spiritual poverty you could ever find—man is empty, poor, helpless. Can he work to earn his own salvation? Is he *penace* poor so he can do just enough to get in "by the hair on his chinny-chin-chin?" No. He is not *penace*. He is *ptokas*.

He's absolutely incapable, totally dependent on grace, and Christ says, "Happy are the destitute, cowering, cringing beggars." What weird news! But let's go on.

"In spirit" means with reference to the inner man, not the body. That's all. He's begging on the inside, not necessarily on the outside. God puts it this way: "But to this one I will look, to him who is humble and contrite of spirit, and who trembles at My word" (Isaiah 66:2). Psalm 34:18 says, "The Lord is near to the brokenhearted, and saves those who are crushed in spirit." Psalm 51:17 says, "The sacrifices of God are a broken spirit; a broken and a contrite heart, O God, Thou wilt not despise."

God identifies with people who beg on the inside, not people who are self-sufficient, not people who think they can work out their own salvation. Poor in spirit does not mean poor-spirited in the sense of lacking enthusiasm. It does not mean lazy or quiet or indifferent or passive. A poor-in-spirit individual is one with no sense of self-sufficiency.

Look at Luke 18 for the best illustration there is of the contrast between the contrite and the proud. It's the story of the Pharisee who was proud of his righteousness and the Publican who begged God's mercy. Luke 18:9 says a mouthful: "And He also told this parable to certain ones who trusted in themselves that they were righteous, and viewed others with contempt." So, how does Jesus conclude this now well-known story? He says of the contrite Publican, "I tell you, this man went down to his house justified rather than the other; for every one that exalts himself shall be humbled, but he who humbles himself shall be exalted" (v. 14).

That's as clear as you'll ever hear it. Blessed are those whose spirit is destitute. Blessed are the spiritual paupers, the spiritually empty, the spiritually bankrupt who cringe in a corner and cry out to God for mercy. They are the happy ones. Why? Because they are the only ones who tap the real resource for happiness. They are the only ones who ever know God. Theirs is the kingdom—then and there, here and now.

This truth is not just in the Sermon on the Mount. James 4:10 says, "Humble yourselves in the presence of the Lord, and He will exalt you." This is not a poverty against which the will rebels, but rather it is a poverty under which the will bows in deep dependence and submission. This is a rather unpopular doctrine in the church today. We emphasize celebrities and experts and superstars and rich, famous Christians. But happiness is for the humble.

Jacob had to face the poverty of spirit before God could use him. He fought God all night, says Genesis 32, and finally God dislocated Jacob's hip. He put him flat on his back. Then, the Bible says in Genesis 32:29, "And he [God] blessed him there." I love that. God made him happy in his humility.

Isaiah could not be used before he was poor in spirit. He lamented the death of King Uzziah and was thinking only of his loss when God graciously invaded the prophet's life and showed him who really mattered. He showed him Himself, high and lifted up in a vision, and Isaiah said, "Woe is me, for I am ruined! Because I am a man of unclean lips . . . for my eyes have seen the King" (Isaiah 6:5). At that point, God blessed him.

Gideon became aware of his inadequacy. He said, "Oh my Lord, wherewith shall I save Israel? behold, my family is poor in Manasseh, and I am the least in my father's house" (Judges 6:15, KJV). God had said, "The LORD is with thee, thou mighty man of valour" (v. 12). You know who the mightiest man of valor is? The man who knows that in himself he is impotent.

That was the spirit of Moses. He was so desperately, horribly, fearfully conscious of his inadequacy and his insufficiency, that God used him to lead His chosen people. It was also the heart of David when he said, "Who am I, O Lord GOD, and what is my house, that Thou hast brought me this far?" (2 Samuel 7:18).

We see it with Peter, aggressive, self-assertive, confident by nature. Yet he said, "Depart from me, for I am a sinful man, O Lord!" (Luke 5:8). The apostle Paul recognized that in his flesh dwelt no good thing. He was the chief of sinners, a blasphemer, a persecutor. Everything he had was garbage. All things he counted loss. He was sufficient for nothing. His strength was made perfect, then, in his weakness.

The world says, "Assert yourself, be proud of yourself, grab your place in the sun." But God says that when you admit your weakness, when you admit your nothingness, that's not the end. It's the beginning! But it is the hardest thing you will ever do. Jesus is saying the first thing you have to admit is, "I can't." That's poverty of spirit. Think about the parable of the unjust servant in Matthew 18. He owed a fortune he could never pay back, an astronomical amount of money. Verse 26 says, "The slave therefore falling down, prostrated himself before him, saying, 'Have patience with me, and I will repay you everything.' " He was saying, "Man, you just hang in there. I've got the resources to do it all!"

Jesus was saying in that parable, "How foolish to say to the Lord, 'Just be patient, I'll do it all.' " Being poor in spirit means being without resources, without pride, without self-assurance, without self-reliance. There must be an emptying before there can be a filling. This is the way to live, not just to get saved, but to *live*.

Before his conversion, St. Augustine was so proud of his intellect that he says it held him back from believing. Only after he emptied himself of his pride did he know God. The great Martin Luther, when he was just a young man, entered a monastery to earn his salvation through piety. When he realized a sense of constant failure after many years, he was forced to recognize his own inability to please God. He emptied himself of himself and based his hope on the salvation provided by God through faith. The Reformation was born.

The only resource for living is for those who know they can't do it. This concept of a standard so high that it cannot be reached in one's self was seen also in the first giving of the law at Sinai. When God gave His law, there were to be no idols, no adultery, no stealing, no murder, and so forth. But even while God was giving it, the people were breaking it below. God was giving it to Moses, and Aaron was leading the people in an orgy. God's standards are not within the realm of man's possibility.

Some of the people of Israel recognized that, so, as God commanded, they gave sacrifices and confessed and came humbly, and God, in His sweet grace, forgave them. But there were others who thought they could do it. While still performing the sacrifices they boasted in their self-righteousness, and they began to try to keep the law in their own strength. They could not do it, but, rather than humbly seeking mercy, they whittled the law down to a series of man-made traditions. Traditions were easier to keep than the law of God.

The Talmudic law, the Jewish law that has grown up around the Torah (the true law of God), is nothing more than a whittled-down standard so that men can have at least some sense of satisfaction. The rabbis said they were trying to protect the law of God, but the fact was they were lowering the requirements to accomodate their self-righteousness. By the time Jesus arrived on the scene, they were doing great with their peripheral stuff while living in daily violation of the true law of God. (See Isaiah 29:13 and Matthew 15:9.)

It's the same with the Sermon on the Mount. This is the law. This is the way to live. But we cannot do it. Yet by the power of the Holy Spirit and dependence on Jesus Christ, we are to desire it. Then we have to deal with our failure in humble contrition and confession. Jesus put the standard up there when He said, "Therefore you are to be perfect, as your heavenly Father is perfect" (Matthew 5:48).

He also said that unless your righteousness exceeds the peripheral, sub-standard, cut down righteousness of the scribes and Pharisees, you are not going to be in His kingdom. The whole intent of law, the purpose of the Sermon on the Mount, as the purpose of Sinai is to show us we can't make it on our own. A lower standard destroys this purpose.

We have to see the majesty of God's law and come to poverty of spirit and total dependence on God in order to fulfill His law. You cannot present these standards to an unregenerate man and expect him to live them. Paul said the function of the law is to render all persons guilty before God, thus driving them to Christ, who alone can remove that guilt. That's the kind of poverty of which Jesus speaks.

What is the result? Simple. "Theirs is the kingdom of heaven." The pronouncement is fantastic. This is not a wish. This is it! Theirs. And, by the way, the pronoun is emphatic, so "theirs *alone*" is the thrust. Who does the kingdom of heaven belong to? Just the poor in spirit. It's a present tense verb. Theirs, mine, ours, yours if you qualify, *is* the kingdom.

We're not just talking about the Millennium. It's yours *now*. There is a future Millennium in which the kingdom promises become full-blown, fully realized, but the kingdom is now. The reign of Christ is now. Happiness is now. The kingdom of heaven is the rule of Christ. It has a future, Messianic aspect; it has a right now aspect. We are now a kingdom of priests. We are now subjects of Jesus Christ. We are now overcomers. We have already, it says in Ephesians 2, been seated together in the heavenly places, the recipient of all of His grace and kindness from now throughout eternity.

The kingdom, as I see it, is grace and glory. Grace now, glory later. We possess the kingdom. It is ours—the rule of Christ, the reign of Christ in our lives. Do you know what that means? We are his subjects, He takes care of us. He gives us what we need. He fulfills every need of our hearts. That's the result of being poor in spirit.

How do we become poor in spirit? You say, "I see the message here. Be poor in spirit. But how do I become poor in spirit?" Let me give you three principles: First, do not begin by trying to do it by yourself. That was the folly of monasticism. They thought they could be poor in spirit by going somewhere, selling all their possessions, putting on a crummy old robe, and sitting in a monastery. It doesn't work. Looking at yourself or even at others will not make it. The place to look is to God.

Read His Word. Face His Person in its pages. Look at Christ. As you gaze at Him and meditate on Him and His Words, you lose yourself. It's not a mystical experience. It's a practical, daily exercise in looking to God. That's principle number one.

Second, starve the flesh. I'm not talking about your diet here; I'm talking about starving your carnal nature. Even some of the Christian ministries of this generation seem to feed on pride. We have to seek things that will strip the flesh naked. It's a fight for me to know this kind of spirit. It's easy for me to accept the accolades, to hear "Thank you, your message blessed me." Or "I was saved when you preached." Or "It's so wonderful at your church." Or "What a wonderful message you gave." It's easy for me to accept compliments. I don't have to struggle with that. But about a year ago I began to hunger in my heart for something that would strip my flesh bare.

I almost found myself wanting to face a folly because I knew it would drive me into the presence of God, and in the presence of God I would be destitute. Not long ago I unintentionally upset some people deeply. My first reaction was that it hurt me because I had not intended to be in error. God began to speak to my heart about the fact that, more than anything, this was what I needed. I needed to face the fact that I was nothing, that in one short breath everything I ever dreamed and desired to do for God (Which, by the way, He doesn't need me to do for Him.) could be taken away.

In my destitution, in my loss, in my failure, in my folly, I gained greater comfort than in anything I had ever been praised for. My fleshly nature had been assaulted and there was no way in the situation to cater to my pride. Though it may sound like self-flagellation, I feel it drew me closer to God than I had been in a long time. It forced me to depend upon Him completely because I had no other resources to deal with my own failure. And that's the place we all want to be—totally dependent upon Him.

The third principle (and this is simple)—ask. Do you want to be poor in spirit? Ask. "God," said the Publican, "be merciful to me." Jesus said that the man went home justified. Happy is the man who is a beggar in his spirit. He's the one who possesses the kingdom.

Why did Jesus begin with this? Because it's the bottom line. It means to be spiritually bankrupt and know it. The result is that you become a possessor of the kingdom, here and now and forever. How do you become poor in spirit? Look at God. Starve your flesh. And ask. Beg. He doesn't mind a bit.

How will I know when I am poor in spirit? Take inventory. Here are seven principles:

• You will be weaned from yourself (Psalm 131:2). One who

is poor in spirit loses a sense of self. It's gone! All you think about is God and His glory and about others and their need.

- You will be lost in the wonder of Christ, "gazing at His glory." (See 2 Corinthians 3:18.) You will be saying, like Philip, "Lord, show us the Father, and is enough for us" (John 14:8). You will be saying with David, "I will be satisfied with Thy likeness when I awake (Psalm 17:5)."

- You will never complain about your situation. Why? You don't deserve anything anyway, right? What have you to offer? In fact, the deeper you go, the sweeter the grace. The more you need, the more abundantly He provides. When you lack everything, you're in a position to receive all grace. There are no distractions. You will suffer without murmur, because you deserve nothing; yet, at the same time, you will seek His grace.

- You will see only the excellencies of others and only your own weaknesses. Truly humble is the one who has to look up to everyone else.

- You will spend much time in prayer. Why? Because a beggar is always begging. He knocks often at heaven's gate, and he doesn't let go until he's blessed.

- You'll take Christ on His terms, not yours. The proud sinner wants Christ and his own pleasure, Christ and his own covetousness, Christ and his own immorality. The one poor in spirit is so desperate that he will give up anything just to get to Christ. Thomas Watson says, "A castle that has long been besieged and is ready to be taken will deliver up on any terms to save its life. He whose heart has been a garrison for the devil and has held out long in opposition against Christ, when once God has brought him to poverty of spirit, and he sees himself damned without Christ, let God prosper, let God offer, and he will simply say, 'Lord, what wilt thou have me to do?' " (Watson, *The Beatitudes, p. 42*).

- Finally, you will praise and thank God for His grace. If

ever there was a characteristic of a person poor in spirit, it is an overwhelming gratitude to God. Every single thing you have is a gift from Him. The beloved apostle Paul says in 1 Timothy 1:14, "The grace of our Lord was more than abundant."

How do we measure up? If we see that we do not measure up at all, we are on our way to true happiness. "Blessed are the poor in spirit."

4

"Happy Are the Sad . . ."

Matthew 5:4

"Blessed are those who mourn,
    for they shall be comforted."
In Psalm 55, one of the great songs of David, he recites the depths of pain that the heart knows in the disappointments and the sorrows of life, and then he cries out, "Oh that I had wings like a dove! I would fly away and be at rest. Behold, I would wander far away, I would lodge in the wilderness. I would hasten to my place of refuge from the stormy wind and tempest" (vv. 6-8).

David echoes a cry of all men at one time or another when they face sorrow, when they face disappointment, when they face tragedy, when they face discouragement. A cry for life on wings, to fly away from the pain and anguish. The deeper the sorrow and disappointment and pain, the more elusive that place of comfort.

That's the paradox of this Beatitude. "Happy are the sad" is contrary to everything we know. The whole structure of our life, the pleasure madness, the thrill seeking, and the money, the energy, the time, the enthusiasm expended in seeking amusement and entertainment are expressions of the world's desire to avoid mourning and sorrow and pain.

Yet Jesus says, "Happy are the sad. Comforted are the mourners." In His offer of a new approach to life, He condemns the laughter and happiness of the world. He pronounces blessing, happiness, joy, peace, and comfort on those who mourn. What in the world does He mean?

The very fact that there are nine different verbs in the Greek alone (all used in Scripture) to express the concept of grief is a pretty good indication that it is a part and parcel of living. The whole of human history is wrought with tears and sorrow, but we haven't seen anything yet, according to Matthew 24.

In that chapter, Jesus says, "See to it that no one misleads you. For many will come in My name, saying, 'I am the Christ,' and will mislead many. And you will be hearing of wars and rumors of wars; see that you are not frightened, for those things must take place, but that is not yet the end. For nation will rise against nation, and kingdom against kingdom, and in various places there will be famines and earthquakes" (vv. 4-7).

Jesus is talking about the end of the age, and He follows it by saying, "All these things are merely the *beginning* of birth pangs"(v.8).

The Bible talks about all different kinds of sorrow and mourning. First, there is what you might call general sorrow, the sorrow of life, a proper kind of sorrow, if you will. This is acceptable, normal weeping and mourning that is part of life. In fact, did you know that the ability to cry is a gift of God? The pain and the anxiety we hold in can poison our entire emotional system if it isn't released in tears.

It's very natural to mourn. Abraham wept when his wife died. In Psalm 42:2-3 the psalmist mourns as his soul pants after God, "My soul thirsts for God, for the living God; when shall I come and appear before God? My tears have been my food day and night, while they say to me all day long, 'Where is your God?' " The grief over the absence of God was released in the heart of the psalmist through the tears that coursed down his cheeks. Loneliness is reason enough to cry.

In 2 Timothy 1:3-4, Paul says to Timothy, "I thank God, whom I serve with a clear conscience, the way my forefathers did, as I constantly remember you in my prayers night and day, longing to see you, even as I recall your tears." Timothy had wept because of discouragement and defeat.

In Jeremiah 9:1, the prophet, who had been called by God to preach to Israel about a coming judgment, came and preached with tears: "O that my head were waters, and my eyes a fountain of tears, that I might weep day and night for the slain of the daughter of my people!"

In Acts 20:31 the apostle Paul told the Ephesian elders, "Therefore be on the alert, remembering that night and day for a period of three years I did not cease to admonish each one with tears."

The psalmist shed tears of loneliness. Timothy shed tears of discouragement. Jeremiah shed tears of disappointment. Paul shed tears of concern. In Mark 9, a father brings his demon-possessed son to Jesus. The tears ran down the father's cheeks as Christ said, " 'If you can!' All things are possible to him who believes" (v. 23). And the father of the child cried out with tears, "I do believe; help my unbelief" (v. 24). Those were tears of earnest love for a son.

In Luke 7 a woman washes Jesus' feet with her tears and dries them with her own hair. Those were tears of devotion, tears of worship, tears of heartfelt gratitude. Love can make people cry. Our Lord wept at the grave of Lazarus because He loved him. He wept over the city of Jerusalem because He loved its people. Mary Magdalene wept because Jesus was dead. Hers were the sorrowing tears of loss, a God-given way to release the terrible pain in your heart.

There is a different kind of weeping. It is improper. It is illicit. It is when a man mourns because he cannot satisfy his lust. This is the tear of Amnon who in 2 Samuel 13 wept and mourned until he became sick, because he wanted to defile his own sister, Tamar. Thus Ahab mourned. He wanted Naboth's vineyard so much that it says in 1 Kings 21:4 he laid on his bed, turned away his face, and would not eat any bread.

Also, sometimes there is the foolish, extended mourning of people who can't let somebody go. You see it often when a person dies and a remaining loved one becomes an emotional basket case. It happens even with Christians now and then. I recently heard of a man who nearly lost his mind because of the loss of his wife who went to be with the Lord. I don't want to sound cold, but that's pure selfishness. It's depressing when one is so selfish that he cannot rejoice in the going to heaven of one he claims to love so deeply. Deep pain and grief over the loss of a life's partner is certainly natural, but this psychotic withdrawing is a whole different matter.

Another kind of illicit sorrow is the kind that's overdone because of guilt. A good biblical illustration of this is found in 2 Samuel 15—20, in which Absalom tries to dethrone his father David. Absalom was proud and egotistical; he particularly liked his hair. He plotted against David and drove him right out of the city of Jerusalem.

Absalom took over the palace and planned a coup that would wipe out David's forces. Unfortunately for Absalom, his side lost, and he was slain. David had told his soldiers, "Deal gently for my sake with the young man Absalom" (2 Samuel 18:5).

When David was told that Absalom was dead, he said, "O my son Absalom, my son, my son Absalom! Would I have died instead of you, O Absalom, my son, my son!" (2 Samuel 18:33). Now his love is admirable, but his idea is stupid. Who wants Absalom to run Israel? Why was David sorrowing like that? Because he was full of guilt over having been such a terrible father, and he hoped his sorrow would wash his own soul from its obvious failures.

No doubt Absalom's death was part of the payment for David's sin with Bathsheba. God had shown him by a parable in 2 Samuel 12 that he would pay four times for that sin. "As the LORD lives," David said, "surely the man who has done this deserves to die. And he must make restitution for the lamb fourfold" (vv. 5-6). God declared through the prophet Nathan, "You are the man!" (v. 7). Four great tragedies came to David: the baby born of Bathsheba died, his daughter Tamar was violated, his son Amnon was slain, and Absalom was slaughtered.

David's mourning over Absalom was so intense that his soldiers were actually ashamed they had won. Joab said, "For I know this day that if Absalom were alive and all of us were dead today, then you would be pleased" (2 Samuel 19:6).

You can see, then, that there are proper and improper kinds of mourning. Some people say, "Well, in general, this Beatitude is true because when you weep you feel a lot better. Sorrow has a way of building you up." But that's not what Jesus is talking about here. He's talking about a godly sorrow that is very different from any of the healthy or unhealthy mourning we have mentioned.

The apostle Paul helps us understand this sorrow in 2 Corinthians 7:10, "For the sorrow that is according to the will of God produces a repentance without regret, leading to salvation; but the sorrow of the world produces death." You can cry your eyes out about your problems, and you can weep all you want about loneliness and about discouragement and about disappointment and out of earnest love, and you can cry your head off about your unfulfilled lust. When it's all said and done, none of that worldly sorrow will bring you life.

Only one kind of sorrow brings life, and that is godly sorrow which leads you to repentance. Therefore, we can conclude that Jesus is referring in this Beatitude to sorrow over sin. That is the issue. Godly sorrow is linked to repen-

tance, and repentance is linked to sin. This kind of mourning means being sorry because you're a sinner.

The Beatitudes began by referring to spiritual bankruptcy
and knowing it. That is the intellectual part. Verse 4 is the
emotional part. Because you know you are spiritually bankrupt, your emotion takes over, and you mourn that bankruptcy. Such are kingdom people. Poor in spirit is a recogni-
tion that we have nothing and that we are nothing and that
we can do nothing, and it results in our being a beggar who
has no resource, no capacity to help himself. What our Lord
is saying in verse 3 is, "Happy is the man who is absolutely
destitute spiritually, who is nothing but a beggar, who has
to plead for mercy and grace, because it's that kind of man
who gets into the kingdom."

As long as we live, we have the same sense of spiritual
poverty. If it was not there at the start, you are not a Christian. If it's not there now, it's questionable whether you are
a Christian. Sound too cold, too rigid, too demanding? The
Bible says being poor in spirit and mourning that fact are
characteristics of kingdom people—Christians.

After David's terrible sin with Bathsheba, and after he
had made sure that Uriah, her husband, was murdered, he
saw not only that in sin had his mother conceived him and
that he was hopeless and poverty-stricken (Psalm 51), but he
also mourned so deeply that it wrenched his soul to its very
depths.

Look at Job. Job had everything. Job was so rich that the
Bible says he washed his doorstep with butter (Job 29:6).
That's rich! Job had everything! But he was never really
made a man until God flattened him and he realized he was
nothing. His response? "Therefore I retract, and I repent in
dust and ashes" (Job 42:6).

The word *mourning* that Jesus has used in this Beatitude is
the strongest, most severe of all nine Greek words used for
grief in Scripture. It is reserved for mourning the dead. It is
used of Jacob's grief when he believed Joseph, his son, was

dead (Genesis 37:34). It's used in the gospels, in Mark 16:10 for example, after the death of Christ when "those who had been with Him . . . were mourning and weeping." The word conveys the idea of a deep inner agony, not just an external wailing.

In Psalm 32 David writes, "When I kept silent about my sin, my body wasted away through my groaning all day long" (v. 3). When David would not confess his sin to God, it tore him up inside. "For day and night Thy hand was heavy upon me; my vitality [blood, lymphatic liquids, saliva, life juices] was drained away as with the fever-heat of summer" (v. 4). Then he says, "I acknowledged my sin to Thee, and my iniquity I did not hide; I said, 'I will confess my transgressions to the Lord'; and Thou didst forgive the guilt of my sin" (v. 5).

In Psalm 51:1-3, reflecting on the same sin with Bathsheba, he said, "Be gracious to me, O God, according to Thy lovingkindness; according to the greatness of Thy compassion, blot out my transgressions. Wash me thoroughly from my iniquity, and cleanse me from my sin. For I know my transgressions, and my sin is ever before me."

In verses 10-12 he continues, "Create in me a clean heart, O God, and renew a steadfast spirit within me. Do not cast me away from Thy presence, and do not take Thy Holy Spirit from me. Restore to me the joy of Thy salvation, and sustain me with a willing spirit." When David mourned his sin and confessed it, he was cleaned out. He had a whole different attitude.

When he got it all out in Psalm 32:1-2, he said, "How blessed is he whose transgression is forgiven [the man who has mourned] whose sin is covered! How blessed is the man to whom the LORD does not impute iniquity."

Mourners are happy because they are the only ones who are forgiven. The rest of the world has to live with that endless guilt. Get it straight now—the happiness does not come from the mourning; it comes in God's response to it.

His response? Comfort. Keep sin in your life and bottle it up, and you'll see how ruinous it becomes. Confess it and see the freedom and the joy that comes in forgiveness.

David had shed tears of loneliness. He had shed tears of rejection. He had shed tears of frustration, discouragement, and disappointment. He had shed tears of defeat. He had even experienced those illicit tears of his own guilt when he tried to atone for his sin. But nothing ever broke the heart of David like his own sin. Then God comforted him, and David said, "How blessed is he whose transgression is forgiven."

Happy are the sad. You know what the world says? "Pack up your troubles in your old kit bag and smile, smile, smile!" The Bible says, "Mourn, mourn, mourn." There's not enough of that, in all honesty. James 4:8-10 says, "Draw near to God and He will draw near to you. Cleanse your hands, you sinners; and purify your hearts, you double-minded. Be miserable and mourn and weep; let your laughter be turned into mourning, and your joy to gloom. Humble yourselves in the presence of the Lord, and He will exalt you."

There's no greater message I can think of for the church today than for it to start crying instead of laughing. It grieves my heart to see the frivolity and the foolishness that goes on in the name of Christianity. Nobody ever came into the kingdom of God who did not mourn over his own sinfulness. You can not verify that you are a true Christian unless throughout your life there is the same sense of grief over the sin in your life.

I can be happy, because I'm forgiven. But I can't enjoy laughter until I've dealt with sin. Even then, it's hard for me to laugh all the time. I know too much to be frivolously happy. God is ready to strike eternal judgment. What are we laughing about?

I fear that the church today has a defective sense of sin. So many people think the Christian life is a joke, that the church is something you make fun of and laugh about. There are people who have set themselves up as satiric critics of the church and spend their time thinking of funny ways to comment on Christianity. One book was recently advertised with the following line: "This book proves that 'the Word of God can be hilarious.' "

Do we laugh when evil is portrayed on television? Do we laugh when we hear about someone doing evil? Do we laugh at jokes about ungodliness? Are those things laughable? Proverbs 2:14 says that some delight in the perverseness of evil. Second Thessalonians 2:12 warns against rejoicing in iniquity. Do we do that? We must not.

I am not against having fun. The Old Testament is pretty clear when it says a merry heart does good like a medicine. But we are so out of balance. We're taking that medicine all the time! It's a far cry from mourning.

Conviction of sin must precede *and follow* conversion. That's the path to blessedness. Some Christians spend all their lives trying to find happiness. They get some counseling and read a book on it when what they really need to do is to mourn their own sin. God will comfort them and Jesus says they'll be blessed (happy), not in the sense of frivolous happiness, but in the sense of a deep and abiding peace born of a right relationship with God.

Some deny their sin, like the Pharisees did, and live a life of deception, trying to make everyone think they're perfect. Others admit their spiritual bankruptcy and then try to change it themselves by saying, "Boy, am I going to go after this one. I'm going to roll up my sleeves and make myself a better person!" Moral rearmament. Others admit their sin and then despair so much that they hang themselves like Judas.

You can deny it and put on a phony front. You can admit it and try to change yourself. You can admit it and sink into despair. Or you can admit it and turn to God for grace and mercy. What did the prodigal son do, way out there in the pig slop? Did he deny his circumstance? "I'm all right! This is really not bad stuff to eat!" Or did he admit he was down and vow to work his way up to respectability on the farm? Did he give up and drown in the slop?

No, he did the right thing. He admitted it and went back to his father where grace and mercy was to be found. He mourned and confessed and was forgiven and comforted and blessed.

Salvation comes by repentance. It comes by mourning. God demands it. There are a lot of folks in this world who think they are Christians, but they have never come to Christ with a bankrupt spirit, mourning their sin. And that's the only way in. The New Testament never talks about making a decision or walking an aisle. It never talks about signing a card. All it says is that you're a Christian if there's present evidence. That's always the issue. In 2 Corinthians 12:21, dear Paul says in effect, if you are not going to cry about it, then all that's left is for me to cry about it.

God demands repentance. He demands realization of sin. I am not talking about wallowing in self-pity. I am talking about genuine repentance. If you don't know the difference, the repentance isn't genuine.

People read Romans 7 and think that Paul's problem with sin was something that happened once in his life and that once he came to live in the truth of Romans 8 he never had a problem with it again. Not true. In Romans 7:15 he says, in essence, "The things I want to do, I don't do, and the things I hate, I do." He says in verses 17-18 that it's "sin which indwells me. For I know that nothing good dwells in me, that is, in my flesh; for the wishing is present in me, but the doing of the good is not." "Sin . . . dwells in me," he says in verse 20. "I find then the principle that evil is present in me, the one who wishes to do good. For I joyfully concur with the law of God in the inner man, but I see a different law in the members of my body, waging war against the law of my mind, and making me a prisoner of the law of sin which is in my members" (vv. 21-23).

Righteousness and sin are fighting. "Wretched man that I am! Who shall set me free from the body of this death?" (v. 24). This is a way of life with him; this is not a one-time encounter. In verse 25 he says, "Thanks be to God through Jesus Christ our Lord!", and people say, "Aha! There it is! The victory!" But just because Paul knew where the victory was doesn't mean it was once for all. He fought it every day of his life till he met Jesus face to face.

John, in 1 John, gives the evidences of a Christian, and one of them is this: If we are confessing our sins, God is faithful and just to forgive us our sins (1:9). What that really means, in context, is this: If we are the ones continually confessing our sins, we give evidence of being the ones who are being forgiven. In other words, the forgiven ones, the subjects of the kingdom, the children of the King, the sons of God, are characterized by constant confession of sin.

Note that in our verse, Matthew 5:4, the verb is a present tense continuous action. The ones continually mourning are continually comforted. Martin Luther, in his 95 Theses, said that our entire life is a continuous act of repentance and contrition. David cried out in Psalm 38:4, "For my iniquities are gone over my head; as a heavy burden they weigh too much for me." He faced sin as a reality all through his life.

One thing we never see Jesus do in the whole New Testament is laugh. He certainly did not have much to laugh about. He was hungry, He was angry, He was thirsty, He wept. But it never says He laughed. We have lost that sobriety. We have been sucked into an entertaining, thrill-seeking, pleasure-mad, silly world of fools and jesters and comedians. But Jesus was a man of sorrows and acquainted with grief. That's what it means to mourn over sin. (Jesus mourned over the sins of others.)

"So, what's mourning going to get me," you ask. "I mope around, sorry for my sin. Then what?" I said before, mourners are not blessed because they mourn. Mourners are blessed because they are comforted. If you don't mourn, you won't get comforted. (By the way, the emphatic pronoun *autoi* is used here, which emphasizes "blessed are they who continue to mourn for they *alone* shall be comforted." Only the mourners know the comfort of God. Only those who mourn their sin know what it is to have their tears dried by the loving hand of Jesus Christ.)

They shall be comforted. Who shall comfort them? *Paraclatos,* from which we get *Paraclete,* the one called alongside to help, the Comforter. The Bible is filled with references to God as a comforter (Psalm 30:5, 50:15, Isaiah 55:6-7, Micah 7:18-20). He helps us, He succors us, He hears our cry, He meets our need, He's always there, beseeching and admonishing and consoling and sympathizing and encouraging and strengthening and forgiving and restoring. That adds up to comfort, the Bible says.

Did you know who the Comforter was? The first was Jesus, because He said, "And I will ask the Father, and He will give you *another* Helper [comforter]" (John 14:16). God is the God of all comfort, Christ the first Paraclete called alongside to help. And the Holy Spirit followed up on the work.

The Word of God is also a comforter. "For whatever was written in earlier times was written for our instruction, that through perseverance and the encouragement of the Scriptures we might have hope" (Romans 15:4). It tells us about God's love, it tells us about His forgiveness, it tells us about His help, and it tells us about his encouragement and presence.

The Holy Spirit comforts us, the Scripture comforts us, and we comfort each other. When we are comforted, we are truly happy. Happiness comes to sad people, not because they are sad, but because their sadness leads to comfort. I love what Jesus said in Matthew 11:28, "Come to Me, all who are weary and heavy-laden, and I will give you rest."

You're not going to come looking for rest unless you know you're heavy-laden, right? Unless you feel your sin. When it's bending your back and weighing you down, then you come and find rest. He takes away your heavy burden and gives you His yoke that is easy and His burden that is light. Carrying on my back the standards of God and the commandments of Christ, while supported by the Holy Spirit, is an easy burden compared to the weight of my sinfulness carried alone.

It comes down to this: We have comfort for as long as we mourn and confess our sin. Then we can truly rejoice.

"How can I become a mourner?"

First, eliminate the hindrances to your realizing sin. Eliminate the things that make your heart hard, that make you resist the Spirit, that make you insensitive. A stony heart does not mourn. It is void of grace. The plow of God will not break it up.

"What makes my heart stony?"

1. *Love of sin.*

2. *Despair.* Do you know what despair says? God can't forgive this! It undervalues God's power and minimizes the blood of Christ. It devalues God's grace and draws God down from the reality of who He is. "But they will say, 'It's hopeless! For we are going to follow our own plans, and each of us will act according to the stubbornness of his evil heart' " (Jeremiah 18:12). In other words, God can't do anything about us anyway, we're beyond hope. The language of despair hides mercy behind ignorance, grace behind doubt. Listen, I don't care how bad it is, how evil you are, God's grace is able to reach you and change you.

3. *Conceit.* "Well, I'm not that bad. If you think I should get sad about what I am, then you don't know me. I'm all right. In fact, I'm pretty good." This is a foolish doctor treating a deadly disease as if it were a cold. If Jesus Christ had to shed His blood and die on a cross for your sin, you are bad. You are very bad, and so am I. If you think you're not bad, you're even worse off, because that's the worst sin of all: pride.

4. *Presumption.* That's cheap grace. "Well, you know, one time I said I wanted Jesus in my heart, and I went down the aisle and got baptized. What do I need to worry about? I'm just going to go ahead and do whatever I want and I'll be all right. I don't need to confess my sin or get upset about anything." But Isaiah 55:7 says, "Let the wicked forsake his way . . . and let him return to the LORD, and He will have compassion on him . . . for He will abundantly pardon." If the wicked does not forsake his way, there is no reason to believe he has any pardon. Don't ever presume. There is no cheap grace. No license.

5. *Procrastination.* "Well, I'm going to have to get around to that one of these days. I'm going to have to get a good look at my sin and really get my act together." James 4:14 says, "You are just a vapor that appears for a little while and then vanishes away." Before you start talking about tomorrow, you'd better realize there may not be a tomorrow. Don't be a fool. The sooner the disease is dealt with, the sooner the comfort comes—and with it the blessedness. Do not put it off. You could spend an eternity without God.

6. *Frivolity.* Some people just do not want to deal realistically with life. They want to laugh all the time. It's just one big party, and as long as they can keep it going, they never have to face the issue. Amos 6:5-7 talks about these unrighteous people and pronounces woe on those "who improvise to the sound of the harp, like David and have composed songs for themselves, who drink wine from sacrificial bowls." A cup isn't enough; they've got to have a bowl of it. "While they anoint themselves with the finest of oils, yet they have not grieved over the ruin of Joseph. Therefore, they will now go into exile at the head of the exiles." You see? Fools! They laugh when there is no cause for laughter. They should be in sorrow.

Our world is mad about parties and music, but one of the first things God is going to do when the whole thing comes down in the Tribulation is to shut off all music. Did you know that? In Revelation 18:22 it says all music is going to stop. People are going to have to face reality. Turn off the radio once in a while. It will help you realize what's really going on inside of you.

"How do I get rid of these hindrances?"

One way is to look at the cross. Understand what Christ did. Christ died for you. If that doesn't break your stony heart, I don't know what will. The poet Christina Rosetti wrote this:

Am I a stone and not a sheep,
that I can stand, O Christ, beneath Thy cross to number drop by drop Thy blood's slow loss and yet not weep?
Not so these women loved who with exceeding grief lamented Thee.
Not so fallen Peter, weeping bitterly. Not so the sun and moon which hid their faces in a starless sky,
a horror of great darkness at broad noon. I, only I. Yet give not o'er. But seek Thy sheep, true Shepherd of the flock.
Greater than Moses, turn and look once more and smite a rock!

If you have hindrances, take a good look at the cross and see how much you need Jesus Christ.

Another way to become a mourner is to study sin in the Scriptures. David said, "I am full of anxiety because of my sin" (Psalm 38:18). Study Isaiah, who said, "Woe is me, for I am ruined! Because I am a man of unclean lips" (Isaiah 6:5). Study Jeremiah, who wept over sin. (See Jeremiah 9.) Study Peter who said, "Depart from me, for I am a sinful man" (Luke 5:8). Study Paul, who said that he was the chief of sinners (1 Timothy 1:15).

When you've compared yourself with these statements by the greatest men who ever lived, you won't be able to convince yourself you're not a sinner. Sin tramples on God's law. Sin slights His love. It grieves His spirit. It spurns His blessedness. Sin affects us drastically. It makes us naked, it makes us impure, it robs our robe and our crown. It spoils our glory. It leaves us in filthy garments. Made in God's image, we become like beasts that perish.

Also, pray for a contrite heart. Only God can give us that. He will not turn down one who really asks.

"How can I know if I'm a mourner?"

Simple. Are you sensitive to sin? Do you laugh at it? Do you let it pass by? Do you take pleasure in it? Maybe it's sin in a moral area, maybe it's dishonesty, maybe it's failure to pray. Maybe it's a failure to think good thoughts, failure to be loving. Do you mourn over your sin?

If we are true mourners, we will mourn not only over our own sin but also over the sins of the world. Do we feel about other people's sin the way the prophet did in Jeremiah 13:17? He said, "But if you will not listen to it, my soul will sob in secret for such pride."

Jesus sits atop the mountain, looks down on Jerusalem, and weeps. He said, "O Jerusalem, Jerusalem. . . ! How often I wanted to gather your children together, the way a hen gathers her chicks under her wings, and you were unwilling" (Matthew 23:37).

Do we weep like that? Is our heart broken when God's heart is broken? Do we say with David in Psalm 69:9, "Zeal for Thy house has consumed me, and the reproaches of those who reproach Thee have fallen on me"? Do we really weep over our sin and the sins around us? If we're mourners, we do.

A second way to know if we're mourners is whether we have a sense of God's forgiveness. Do we know joy in our lives? Do we know real peace, real happiness, real comfort that comes to a forgiven, cleansed, purified life?

I hope you are a mourner, because God wants you to be comforted. He wants you to be genuinely happy.

5

"Happy Are the Meek . . ."

Matthew 5:5

"Blessed are the gentle, for they shall inherit the earth."

The King James translates this verse "Blessed are the meek: for they shall inherit the earth." This was a shocking statement to Jesus' audience. It was absolutely foreign to their thinking.

They knew how to be spiritually proud.

They knew how to be self-sufficient.

They knew how to play the pious role.

They knew religion.

They were really good with form.

They thought they were the "in" group.

They thought they could survive on their own strength and wisdom and might and resources.

And when the Messiah arrived they expected Him to usher them into His kingdom and say, "I'm here to commend you for your religiosity, for your wonderful spirituality. God has looked down from heaven and He's very well-pleased with you."

They didn't understand this revolutionary approach. They had banked everything on their spirituality, and Jesus undermined it all the first time He opened His mouth. He called for a broken spirit, a mourning heart, and now meekness. No self-righteousness, no spiritual pride.

Our society is not unlike theirs. We think the victory and the spoils belong to the strong. Go get it! Gusto! Macho! Perhaps we're as jolted by Jesus' new approach as the Jews were. Let's set the scene and see where in their history Jesus appeared to the Jews.

A little over half a century before Jesus was born, Pompei annexed Palestine to Rome in 63 B.C., and Jewish independence ended. That independence had been gained from Greece in a blood-bath rebellion called the Maccabean Revolt, but it was not very long before they were under the bondage of the imperial power of Rome.

From 63 B.C., the land was ruled partly by Herodian kings (a family of monarchs appointed by Caesar). Caesar gave the people in Palestine kings because they wanted kings, but, in addition, he gave them procurators and governors, the most famous of whom was Pontius Pilate. While the Jews were under the Roman domination of those puppet Herodian kings, procurators, and governors, virtually all other land with which the New Testament is concerned was also under Rome.

It was a sad day for Jewish people. They despised that Roman oppression so much that they would not even admit they were under it. When Jesus told the Jewish leaders in John 8:32 that "You shall know the truth, and the truth shall make you free," they answered, "We are Abraham's offspring, and have never yet been enslaved to anyone" (v. 33).

The whole story of Jesus falls within the framework of a nation in bondage to Rome. The shadow of Caesar falls over the New Testament and we can feel him on every page. At the same time, there was a movement in the hearts of the Jews to believe the Messiah was coming. There was the feeling that something was about to happen. The kingdom of God would be established, the Scriptures were clear on that.

Then this Jesus arrives on the scene, and look what Mark tells us He said, starting with Mark 1:14. "And after John had been taken into custody, Jesus came into Galilee, preaching the gospel of God, and saying, 'The time is fulfilled, and the kingdom of God is at hand; repent and believe in the gospel.' "

They got excited! They had known Roman domination and oppression, and now, all of a sudden, here came a wonder worker, a miracle-man, someone who spoke like never another man spoke. Maybe this really was the Messiah!

When he fed the multitude on the side of the hill, they wanted to make Him a king and begin a revolution that would throw off the yoke of Rome. They were looking for a great leader who could set up a revolution that would bring about independence. Remember that there were four basic parties in Judaism at that time: Pharisees, Sadducees, Zealots, and Essenes.

The Pharisees were the religious conservatives, and the Sadducees were the liberals. The Essenes were the mystics who lived out in Qumran where the Dead Sea Scrolls were found. The Zealots were the activists who were concerned more about politics than religion. Theirs was a military kingdom dream. The were looking for a general to lead a military revolution.

The Pharisees were equally anxious to overthrow Rome, but they weren't looking for a military kingdom. They were looking for a holy commonwealth, a restoration of the Old Testament theocracy. They were looking for a miraculous Messiah who would throw off Rome by some great supernatural act. Both the Pharisees and the Zealots were awaiting a catastrophic intervention of God. They knew the Scriptures said in Daniel 7:13-14 that the Messiah would come in clouds and great glory, and while they did not know how it would happen, each had their own ideas.

Even the twelve apostles expected it. In Acts 1:6 they ask, "Lord, is it at this time You are restoring the kingdom to

Israel?" They wanted to know when they were going to see either the miraculous or the military action. But this was not Jesus' purpose, and that's why in John 18 when Pilate was trying to figure out what kind of a king does not have a kingdom, a throne, or a crown, Jesus said, "My kingdom is not of this world" (v. 36). He was saying, in effect, "You don't understand what kind of king I am. It isn't my approach to function militarily. I'm not about to pull off a miraculous coup and overthrow Rome. That's not my purpose." If He had wanted to, He could have called legions of angels, thousands of them. (If one angel can slay 185,000 Assyrians in one shot [2 Kings 19:35], a legion of angels could handle anything.)

The hope of a political and religious restoration was a pipe dream, but it so burned in Jewish hearts that it produced false messiahs like a rash. They were everywhere. False messiahs by the boatload.

The Zealots could not wait for the Messiah, so along with the *sicarii,* who were the assassins in their ranks, they would strike at Rome. They would assassinate some important person or pull off some other revolutionary act, and all it did was bring about Roman reprisals.

So, God's plan was not what the Jews thought it would be, and when Jesus started talking the way He did in the Sermon on the Mount, you can imagine their reaction. "What kind of messiah is this? What kind of a crowd is He going to collect? Who wants a bunch of sob sisters, a bunch of meek people? They'll never handle Rome!"

He so disappointed the political activists because He would not pull off a revolution, and the religionists because He did not destroy Rome with a cataclysmic miracle. When they finally saw Him captured by the Romans, and standing next to Barabbas as a pathetic person whom Pilate had battered and beaten and bruised and scourged and crowned with a crown of thorns, there was no beauty in Him that man should desire Him (Isaiah 53). So they thought, *Forget it! That's not the Messiah we want.* And they cried, "Crucify Him! Crucify Him!"

They hated Him because He disappointed them and did not fulfill their expectations. When people later said, "He was the Messiah," they said, "Look, He died on a cross. The Old Testament says 'cursed is everyone that hangs on a tree.' Don't tell us He is our Messiah!" (See Deuteronomy 21:23 and Galatians 3:13.)

Although five hundred people testified to the resurrection, the disappointed Jews would not believe it. The apostles had to preach always on the resurrection, and they had to say always, "You see, Messiah had to suffer. He had to die. This is what the Scripture taught. It had to be this way." Jesus, on the road to Emmaus, said, "If you had known the Scriptures, you'd have known it had to happen this way." (See Luke 24:25-27.)

But most Jews were ignorant of the significance of Isaiah 40-66, the huge section that presents the Messiah as a suffering servant. In fact, when He announced who He really was, He quoted Isaiah 61. He identified with a low crowd. He said, "The Spirit of the LORD is upon Me, because he anointed Me to preach the gospel to the poor . . . to proclaim release to the captives, and recovery of sight to the blind, to set free those who are downtrodden, to proclaim the favorable year of the LORD" (Luke 4:18). Now that's a pretty sad bunch!

The apostle Paul said in 1 Corinthians 1:26-27, "Not many wise according to the flesh, not many mighty, not many noble; but God has chosen the foolish things of the world." He was a servant. He did not come to overthrow Rome. He came to wash the feet of unloving disciples. His whole life was an illustration of humility and service. He said, "For even the Son of Man did not come to be served, but to serve, and to give His life a ransom for many" (Mark 10:45).

They missed the whole point. They didn't know what He came for. Humility. Self-denial. He was saying that "It's not the self-sufficient, the self-righteous, the proud, the strong, the arrogant, the confident, and the religious who enter My kingdom. It is the broken and the mourning and the meek and the hungry and the thirsty and the merciful and the pure and the peacemakers and the persecuted and the reviled and the slandered who never retaliate. They're the citizens of My kingdom."

They couldn't believe it. Sometimes neither can we. We think God needs superstars. We think God needs the high and the mighty, the rich and the famous. It's never been that way! Our Lord came and hit them right where they were hurting. He said, "Look, do you want to be in my kingdom? The ones in My kingdom are spiritually bankrupt, mournful, and meek."

Now, let's talk in detail about meekness.

It's different from being broken in spirit, though the root word is the same. In some places in the Bible these words could be used interchangeably, but I like to see a beautiful distinction. Broken in spirit focuses on my sinfulness. Meekness focuses on God's holiness.

In other words, I am poor in spirit because I am a sinner, and meek because God is so holy in comparison. Broken in spirit is negative and results in mourning. Meekness is positive and results in seeking righteousness. That's the beauty of the sequence, of the progression in the Sermon on the Mount. First there's the brokenness, the tremendous sense of sinfulness. But there is no despair because you begin to see the other side of it. You see a holy God and begin to hunger after His holiness.

People who are realistic and repentant about their sin are responsive to God. And the unblessed and unhappy and those shut out of the kingdom are the arrogant, self-sufficient, self-righteous, unrepentant, stiff-necked, proud people. This was devastating.

The Zealots were saying, "We want a military messiah." The Pharisees were saying, "We want a miraculous messiah." The Sadducees were saying, "We want a materialistic messiah." And the Essenes were over in the corner saying. "We want a monastic messiah." But Jesus said, "I'll give you a meek one."

Many of the apostle Paul's New Testament letters parallel this teaching. In Ephesians 4:1-2 (KJV) he says, "I therefore, the prisoner of the Lord, beseech you that ye walk worthy of the vocation wherewith ye are called, with all lowliness and meekness." Titus 3:2 (KJV), "Speak evil of no man, to be no brawlers, but gentle, shewing all meekness unto all men." Colossians 3:12 (KJV), "Put on, therefore, as the elect of God, holy and beloved, bowels of mercies, kindness, humbleness of mind, meekness."

God's standard has always been the same. You see meekness all the way back in the Old Testament. Psalm 22:26 (KJV) says, "The meek shall eat and be satisfied: they shall praise the LORD that seek him: your heart shall live for ever." Everlasting life belongs to the meek, not the proud. Psalm 25:9 (KJV), "The meek will He guide in judgment: and the meek will he teach his way." Psalm 147:6 (KJV), "The LORD lifteth up the meek."

God has always identified with the meek. They are a priority with Him. They are His kind of people. Isaiah 29:19 (KJV), "The meek also shall increase their joy in the LORD." Salvation and teaching and blessing and joy for the meek.

Now, let's cover five obvious questions about meekness.

What does it really mean to be meek?

If the only happy people are the meek, we had better learn what meekness is. Whatever it is, it comes out of those hearts that are poor in spirit and mourning. The dictionary definition of meekness, "deficient in courage," is not the Bible's definition. The scriptural *meek* comes from a Greek word, *praos,* and it means, basically, "mild, gentle, and soft."

So, a meek person is someone who is gentle, mild, tenderhearted, patient, submissive. *Meek* was often used to describe a soothing medicine, a gentle breeze, a colt that had been broken and domesticated. Further, it was a characteristic of Jesus. Second Corinthians 10:1 and Matthew 21:5 talk about the meekness of Christ. The latter says, "Behold, thy King cometh unto thee, meek, and sitting upon an ass, and a colt the foal of an ass" (KJV).

When Jesus came into the city, He was riding not on a white charger but on the foal of a donkey. That was really low-class transportation. He was meek. Meekness is a gentleness and a mildness, and a subdued character, but it is not weakness. It is power under control. Get that definition. Power under control. It is a by-product of self-emptying, of self-humiliation, of brokenness before God. It is the taming of the lion.

Meekness does not mean impotence. Proverbs 25:28 says, "Like a city that is broken into and without walls is a man who has no control over his spirit." In other words, you've got power but no control over it. It's like a destroyed city. On the other hand, Proverbs 16:32 says, "He who is slow to anger is better than the mighty, and he who rules his spirit than he who captures a city." To rule the spirit is meekness. To be out of control is to lack meekness.

Let's look at *meek* from the standpoint of the Greeks' use of it. An unbroken colt destroys. A broken colt is useful. A gentle breeze cools and soothes. A hurricane kills. Meekness is the opposite of violence and vengeance. The meek man has learned to take joyfully the plundering of his possession, knowing that he has a better possession. even an abiding one, with God (Hebrews 10:34). The meek person has died to self. He never worries about his own injuries. He bears no grudges.

I think it was John Bunyan who said, "He who is already down cannot fall." There's nothing to lose. A meek person never defends himself because he knows he doesn't deserve anything. He never gets angry about what's done to him.

He's not running around trying to get his due. He's already broken in spirit over his sin, and he's already mourning and weeping over the consequence of it. In humility he stands before a holy God and he has nothing to commend himself.

It isn't cowardice, it isn't flabbiness, it isn't wishy-washy lack of conviction. It isn't just human niceness. Meekness says, "In myself, nothing is possible. But in God, everything is possible." Meekness says, "For me, I offer no defense. For God, I'll give my life." It is not passive acceptance of sin; it is anger under control. It is holy indignation.

Consider 1 Peter 2:21, "For you have been called for this purpose, since Christ also suffered for you, leaving you an example for you to follow in His steps, who committed no sin, nor was any deceit found in His mouth." Now there's real meekness. He never did anything wrong, so whatever anybody accused Him of was false. Whatever anybody punished Him for was wrong. Whenever they abused Him, they were out of line. Whenever they slandered Him, they were wrong. Whenever they mocked Him, it was a lie.

Two verses later in that same 1 Peter passage, when He was reviled, "He did not revile in return; while suffering, He uttered no threats, but kept entrusting Himself to Him who judges righteously."

That's meekness. And to such a one God promises the earth. Jesus never defended Himself, but when they desecrated His Father's Temple, He made a whip and beat them. Meekness says, "I'll never defend myself, but I'll die defending God." Twice Jesus cleansed the Temple. He blasted the hypocrites. He condemned false leaders of Israel. He fearlessly uttered divine judgment upon people. And yet the Bible says He was meek. Meekness is power used only in the defense of God.

How does meekness manifest itself?

Remember in Genesis 12 when God gave Abraham the fabulous covenant? "You're going to have seed like the stars of heaven and the sand of the sea. Abraham, I'm going to give you a land. Abraham, I'm going to give you a covenant that is like no covenant ever given. Out of your loins is going to come a nation." (See vv. 1-3.)

A chapter later we read of strife between the herdsmen of Abraham's cattle and the herdsmen of his nephew Lot's cattle. Abraham could have said, "Look, Buster! Who got the covenant? You or me?"

"Well, you did, Uncle Abraham."

"And don't you forget it, Sonny! I got the covenant, so I get the pick of the land!" He could have pulled rank. He had the right. He was God's man. Lot was nothing but a hitchhiking relative. So, how did Abraham deal with it? Look at Genesis 13.

"Then Abram said to Lot, 'Please let there be no strife between you and me, nor between my herdsmen and your herdsmen, for we are brothers. Is not the whole land before you? Please separate from me: if to the left, then I will go to the right; or if to the right, then I will go to the left' " (13:8-9). In other words, "You take whatever portion you want, and I'll take what's left." That's meekness. When you see that you are nothing more than a sinner, you will learn the meaning of Romans 12:10, "give preference to one another in honor," as Abraham did.

Then there was Joseph. His brothers sold him into slavery and he was taken down into Egypt. They thought, *We are rid of that kid.* They couldn't tolerate him because their father doted on him. Then later there was famine and they had to go to Egypt to get grain. Guess who was the key man in Egypt? Joseph. He had risen to the rank of prime minister next to the Pharaoh, and here were his brothers begging him for grain.

He could have said, "Let me tell you a little story before I say no." But he didn't. He had the power, but it was under control. There was not a vengeful bone in his body. There was no antagonism or bitterness, no grudge. He loved them and he gave them everything they needed. In fact, he noticed that Benjamin wasn't there, and he longed to see Benjamin. Joseph was no coward; he had squared off with Pharaoh. Joseph was a mighty man. Meekness is not cowardice.

Remember in 1 Samuel 26 when Saul was chasing David? Saul knew that God had anointed David to be the next king. Saul hated him and tried to kill him, but when David suddenly came upon Saul and found him sound asleep, the tables were turned. This was David's opportunity. David's men said to him, "Do it, David. Do it. Get him! I mean, he's here, man! This is your time! Don't mess around, David. You let him go and you're going to get it yourself!"

David took Saul's spear and water jug just so that Saul would know he had been there and that he could have killed him. David did not use his power. He had the spear and Saul was asleep, but he did not do it. He would not act on his own behalf, but he would act on behalf of God.

In 2 Samuel 16 David and his son Absalom were in conflict and Absalom chased David out of Jerusalem. One of Saul's former henchmen named Shimei came along and cursed David. "Look at you," he snarled. "Your son has knocked you off, David. Hot shot, aren't you? Big stuff! Big king of Israel, out here hiding in the bush!"

Abishai, David's nephew, said, "Let me go over there and cut his head off, David. Who does he think he is, cursing the king?" But David told him to leave Shimei alone. He would not act in his own defense. At that moment he had a beautiful, subservient, trusting attitude of total submission to God's will.

Numbers 12:3 says Moses was meek above all the men who were on the face of the earth. You say, "Meek? *He* was meek?" He was the one who told Pharaoh, "Let my people go!" He was the one who came down out of Mt. Sinai and saw his brother leading the people in the worship of the golden calf and the people having an orgy. He was so furious that he smashed the tablets of stone. True, but he was not defending himself. He was defending the Lord God.

In fact, when God had said to him (Exodus 3), "Moses, you're My man," Moses replied, "You don't want me, God, I'm useless. I'm inadequate. I have a speech impediment. You've got to be kidding. You want me to lead children of Israel out of Egypt? I killed one Egyptian and it's cost me forty years in the wilderness! How am I going to get two million Jews out of that country without a lot of trouble? I can't do it."

He had no confidence in himself. He could not defend himself before God, but he would defend God before anybody. That's meekness.

Paul said in Philippians 3:3 that he could put no confidence in the flesh." But look at Philippians 4:13, "I can do all things through Him [Christ] who strengthens me."

What is the result of meekness?

Blessed are the meek. That's the first result. Do you want to be happy *(makarios)*? That's what it means. Not happiness in the sense of the world's flippant, circumstantial kind of happiness, but happiness in God's terminology—an abiding, true joy, based on an eternal relationship with the living God.

Second, and this is great, the meek shall inherit the earth. What Christ means here is that when you enter the kingdom, you come into the original inheritance of dominion over the earth that God gave to Adam. It's paradise regained. The people in the kingdom shall inherit the earth. The only ones who enter His kingdom are the ones who are broken over their sin, not the ones who think they have no sin. The ones who are mourning over the fact that they're lost, not the ones who are laughing about the fact that they are supposedly all right.

In Genesis, God promised His children the land. Do you realize that the original promise extends all the way to the Euphrates River? The Jews can hardly get across the Jordan to the East Bank, so there's a sense in which that is an unfulfilled promise. Isaiah 57:13 and 60:21 say that there's going to come a day when Messiah comes and He's going to give them all that land, and the whole earth, too.

But you know what the Jews of Jesus' day thought?

"The Millennial kingdom belongs to the strong. The proud. The defiant. Those who won't take this oppression."

Jesus said, "No, no, no. The earth will belong to the meek." How are the meek going to pull it off, how will they get it? Well, they won't. They don't do anything. Christ does it. The meek go into the kingdom, and Christ gives them the earth. The emphatic pronoun is used here again as in the other Beatitudes, so it says in Greek, "Blessed are the meek, for they *only* shall inherit the earth."

The word *inherit* in the Greek means "to receive an allot-ted portion." God promised it. God laid it out. In Psalm 37 there was a very definite promise of the land, and yet the righteous among the Jews were saying, "Well, why do all the evil people prosper while we are getting the dirty end of everything?"

The psalmist responds, in effect, "Don't you worry about that. You just commit your way to the Lord, trust also in Him, delight in Him, and He will give you the desires of your heart." Psalm 37:13 says the Lord "laughs at him; for He sees his day is coming." It may look like it's reversed now, but He says those people, those evildoers, shall be cut down like the grass, and they shall wither like the green herb. "For evildoers will be cut off, but those who wait for the LORD, they will inherit the land". (v. 9).

Inherit is a future tense verb. We're going to be there as part of that kingdom. We're going to reign with Jesus Christ. In 1 Corinthians 3:21-23 it says, "So then let no one boast in men. For all things belong to you, whether Paul or Apollos or Cephas or the world or life or death or things present or things to come; all things belong to you, and you belong to Christ; and Christ belongs to God."

Psalm 149:4 (KJV) says, "For the LORD taketh pleasure in his people: he will beautify the meek with salvation." One day He will execute vengeance on the nations. He will bind their kings with chains and their nobles with fetters. One of these days He's going to gather up the wicked, take it all away from them, and give the new earth to His own. The world as I know it now, the world as I see it now, comes alive with meaning for me because it's mine, in escrow. The fact that I'm in His kingdom helps me see it differently. Apart from Christ, I could never see it any other way than the way the world sees it. And someday it will be mine in the fullness of millennial promise.

Why is meekness necessary?

Only the meek can be saved. Psalm 149:4 (KJV), "He will beautify the meek with salvation." If you do not come to God with a broken spirit, mourning over your sin in humility before His holiness, you cannot be saved. Further, it is commanded. In Zephaniah 2:3 (KJV), God says, "Seek meekness."

You need meekness because you can't even receive God's Word without it. James 1:21 (KJV) says, "Receive with meekness the engrafted word." Neither can you witness without meekness. Did you know that? That's why Peter says, "Give an answer to every man that asketh you a reason of the hope that is in you with meekness and fear" (1 Peter 3:15, KJV).

Also, you need to be meek because meekness alone gives God the glory. In 1 Peter 3:4, Peter says if you want to glorify God, don't take care of your outside, but adorn your inside with meekness.

So, meekness is necessary because it's the only way to be saved, it's commanded by God, it's necessary for receiving and giving out His Word, and it's the very reason for existence—to glorify God.

How do I know if I'm meek?

Examine your heart. Do you exhibit self-control? Do you get angry, do you react, or do you retaliate only when God is dishonored?

Do you always respond humbly and obediently to the Word? If you're meek, you will.

Do you always make peace? Meekness forgives and restores. That's why Ephesians 4:2-3 says we are to be characterized with all lowliness and meekness, endeavoring to keep the unity of the Spirit in the bond of peace.

Do you receive criticism well and love the people who give it? Meekness does. Do you give instruction with meekness?

Meekness means to be finished with *me* for good.

6

"Happy Are the Hungry. . ."

Matthew 5:6

"Blessed are those who hunger and thirst for righteousness, for they shall be satisfied."

Keep in mind that the overall theme of Matthew is Christ as King. Repeatedly, Matthew emphasizes some element of the kingliness of Christ, whether it's a kingly line in His genealogy, the worship of the magi (the official, oriental king makers), the fulfilling of the kingly prophecies of the Old Testament, or the dominion He has over Satan. In any case, Matthew presents Christ as King.

In chapter five he presents the words of the King, or the manifesto of the kingdom. If indeed Christ is a king, of what nature is His kingdom? He describes it in Matthew 5, 6, and 7, and we recognize immediately that it is a spiritual kingdom. At the very end of the Sermon on the Mount, in Matthew 7:28, it says, "The result was that when Jesus had finished these words, the multitudes were amazed at His teaching." Why? "For He was teaching them as one having authority, and not as their scribes" (Matthew 7:29).

Not only were His words the words of a king, but His way was also the way of a king. His was the manner of a king. He was authoritative. He did not need to quote anybody. The

rabbis and scribes always taught by quoting somebody famous. Jesus simply said it.

Jesus introduced His sermon by saying that it's happiness
He's after, it's blessedness He's offering. But His presenta-
tion was not exactly what they expected. He offered them a
happiness that they had never known and in a way that they
had never before heard it, and consequently, it fascinated
them. By the time He was finished, they were more than
fascinated, they were astonished.

Let me interject an important clarification. People ask,
"Are the truths in the Beatitudes the rules on how you get
into the kingdom, or are they rules on how you live once
you're in the kingdom?" The answer is yes. Both. To enter
the kingdom you must be poor in spirit. As you live in the
kingdom you continue to recognize your spiritual poverty.
To enter the kingdom you must mourn over your sin, and as
you continue in the kingdom you will mourn over your sin.
To enter the kingdom you must come in meekness. A proud
man cannot enter. Once you're in the kingdom, meekness
continues to be your attitude as God becomes more and
more wonderful to you. To enter the kingdom you must
hunger and thirst after righteousness. And once you're in
the kingdom, you'll continue to do the same. Obviously,
there will be times when we are less faithful and sometimes
downright disobedient to these elements of kingdom life.
But they are still a part of our life.

Our verse for this chapter of study speaks of a very strong
desire, a driving pursuit, a passionate force inside us, an
ambition. There are plenty of biblical examples of people
who were hungry for the wrong thing. There is Lucifer,
Nebuchadnezzar, and the rich fool, among others. But
there's nothing wrong with ambition, passion, a resolute
drive, or great desire, if it focuses on the right thing.

What is the right thing? Go back to verse 6: "Blessed are
those who hunger and thirst for righteousness." This is a
strong statement. Food and water are necessities, and here

Christ is saying you need righteousness like you need food. Our physical life depends on food and water; our spiritual life depends on righteousness.

Today, in parts of Africa, India, and Latin America, thousands die of malnutrition and its accompanying diseases. Hunger is like war and pestilence. It kills. It consumes. But all the hunger horrors imaginable grow pale when compared to the horror of unfulfilled spiritual hunger and unquenched spiritual thirst.

Unsaved people thirst for happiness and hunger for fulfillment, but they seek it in the wrong places. In fact, Peter compares the unsaved to a dog that licks up its own vomit or a pig that wallows in its own mire. (See 2 Peter 2:22.) The heart of every person in the world, believer or unbeliever, was created with a hunger for God. But man tries to satisfy hunger for God with all the wrong things. He seeks what the Scripture calls "what is not bread" (Isaiah 55:2).

Jesus knew people were hungry and offered Himself as bread. He knew they were thirsty and offered Himself as water. Yet, Jeremiah described the people's common reaction vividly in Jeremiah 2:13, "They have forsaken Me, the fountain of living waters, to hew for themselves cisterns, broken cisterns, that can hold no water."

First John 2:15-16 warns that you won't find satisfaction in the world. "Do not love the world, nor the things in the world. . . . the lust of the flesh and the lust of the eyes and the boastful pride of life." None of that abides forever. It's just wind. Those who respond to the Spirit of God come running back to the Father, and there is a feast to fill the empty heart.

So, right at the start, ask yourself, What am I hungry for? Power? Praise? Possessions? Pleasure? Are you like the dog who licks his own vomit? The pig that wallows in his own mire? Or are you looking to the real source? Your answer will determine whether or not you are in the kingdom. The blessed hunger and thirst after righteousness.

Some key questions face us here, as they have for each of the Beatitudes.

How does this Beatitude fit in with the others?

We talked about the fact that the "poor in spirit" of verse three means recognizing that you are destitute of any righteous thing and morally bankrupt. We cannot help ourselves. We are hopeless. We are sinful. And that is followed by, "they that mourn." That is the response to your broken spirit: mourning. Then there is meekness, and meekness says, "In comparison to God, I am nothing!" Meekness is humility. In our meekness before God, we realize that the only hope we ever have of knowing righteousness is to seek it at His hand. That brings us to the fourth Beatitude, and we hunger and thirst after what we know is not ours.

So the progression is simple. Martyn Lloyd-Jones writes,
> This Beatitude follows logically from the previous one. See, it is a statement to which all the others lead. It is the logical conclusion to which they come. It is something for which we should all be profoundly thankful and grateful to God. I do not know of a better test that anyone can apply to himself or herself in this whole matter of the Christian profession, than a verse like this. If this verse is to you one of the most blessed statements of the whole of Scripture, you can be quite sure you're a Christian. If it is not, you had better examine your foundations again. [Martyn Lloyd-Jones, *Studies in the Sermon on the Mount* (Grand Rapids: Eerdmans, 1959), 1:73-74.]

Jesus says happiness is brokenness, happiness is mourning, happiness is meekness, happiness is hungering and thirsting after righteousness. Notice how the result of each of those fit together. "Theirs is the kingdom of heaven, they shall be comforted, they shall inherit the earth, they shall be satisfied." Isn't that fabulous? If we sum that all up, we receive everything there is!

In other words, on God's condition, everything is going to be ours. The world is working furiously to gain things, yet if it came into God's kingdom on His terms, it would get it all anyway. People are breaking their necks to get what God wants to give! (See James 4:1-2.)

The Jews were working to bring on the kingdom. They were doing their best to be comforted in a very difficult situation, and they intensely wanted to inherit the earth. They were trying to fill up their lives with meaning. They were chasing the wrong way and the Lord simply said to them, "I'll give you everything you want. I'll give you the kingdom, I'll give you comfort, I'll fill your life with everything you need, I'll give you the whole earth. You can have the whole deal if you'll just come on My conditions."

Once we believe God's promise, we don't have to work, we inherit. I read my Bible this way: God says, "You're my child. You'll inherit the earth." So why should I spend all my time trying to gain it on my own? It doesn't make any sense. It's going to be mine anyway. I don't mind other people borrowing it for a while. It's all coming back to me, based on His promise.

Isaac went from well to well to well. Every time he dug a well, somebody contested ownership and took it away from him. Finally, he dug a well that nobody contested and he named it, "Rehoboth, for he said, 'At last the LORD has made room for us' " (Genesis 26:22). He knew God would take care of him. He could be unselfish. This is the whole basis of motivation in the Sermon on the Mount.

It can only become yours at His hand. This then becomes the motivation for other things. Matthew 5:40 says, "If any one wants to sue you, and take away your shirt, let him have your coat also." Why? Because you have all you need in the kingdom. What do you care? "And whoever shall force you to go one mile, go with him two. Give to him who asks of you, and do not turn away from him who wants to borrow from you" (Matthew 5:41-42). Listen, don't hang on to the stuff of the world. It'll all be yours anyway. So share it. With that kind of heart, with that kind of spirit, you can have the right ambition.

If you're saying, "Look, all I want, God, is Your righteousness. All I want is to be meek before You. All I want is to have Your kingdom on Your terms," His promise is that you shall inherit everything in the end. Everything! In fact, the apostle Paul even said to the Corinthians, "All things belong to you," (1 Corinthians 3:22-23 and you belong to Christ; and Christ belongs to God"). It's all yours anyway!

Jesus said it this way in Matthew 6:33: "But seek first His kingdom and His righteousness; and all these things shall be added to you." It's all ours anyway, on God's terms, so we can say, "Happy are the hungry."

There's pain in verse 3, "broken in spirit"; there's pain in verse 4, "mourning"; there's pain in verse 5, "meekness" (the death of self). But after the pain of hungering and thirsting, there's comfort in verse 6, because we have come to the place where we are reaching out to God. That's why this Beatitude fits here. Because it makes sense.

What does it mean to hunger and thirst?

We have already hinted at what it means to hunger and thirst. It has to do with desire, a great and intense desire. The force of Christ's words here is powerful, particularly in that culture. We do not really know what it is to be hungry or to thirst. When we think of thirst we think of simply going to the available source when we want something to drink. When we say we're hungry, we mean it's 1:00 p.m. and we've used to eating at 12:15.

James Boice relates the following account about a famous military leader, Major V. Gilbert, who tells in his book, *The Last Crusade*, of the thirst he and his men suffered in the Palestinian desert in World War I.

> "Our heads ached. Our eyes became bloodshot and
> dim in the blinding glare. . . . Our tongues began to

swell. . .our lips turned to a purplish black and burst.
Those who dropped out of the column were never seen
again, but the desperate force battled on to Sheria.
There were wells at Sheria, and had they been unable to
take the place by nightfall, thousands were doomed to
die of thirst.

"We fought that day as men fight for their lives. We
entered Sheria's station on the heels of the retreating
Turks. The first objects which met our view were the
great stone cisterns full of cold, clear drinking water. . . . It took four hours before the last man had his
drink of water. . . . I believe that we all learned our first
real Bible lesson on that march from Beersheba to the
Sheria wells. If such were our thirst for God and for
righteousness, for His will in our lives, a consuming,
all-embracing, preoccupying desire, how rich in the
fruit of the Spirit would we be." [*Eternity*, August 1966.]

Jesus was talking about hunger and thirst to people who
understood this kind of want. The Greek verbs are very
powerful. *Peinao* means to be needy, to suffer deep hunger.
The word *dipsao* carries the idea of genuine thirst. Jesus puts
the strongest physical impulses in a continuous action,
present participle—the ones who *are* hungering, the ones
who *are* thirsting. Remember, this is not the requirement
only of the one coming into the kingdom, but also the pattern of the one already in.

When I came to Jesus Christ, I hungered and thirsted for
His righteousness, and now that I know Him, I hunger and
thirst for more of it. R. C. H. Lenski, the great commentator,
says, "This hungering and this thirsting continues and, in
fact increases in the very act of being satisfied." (R. C. H.
Lenski, *The Interpretation of Matthew's Gospel* [Minneapolis:
Augsburg], p. 189.) It is a moment-by-moment way of life. If
you do not hunger and thirst for righteousness, there is a
question whether you are even in the kingdom.

Let me use Moses as an illustration. When he had been in

the wilderness for forty years, God called him. He saw God in the burning bush. When Moses went back to lead Israel out of the land, he saw God's hand in the plagues and in the parting of the Red Sea. He saw God as they moved, guided by the great Shekinah glow of God in the heavens. He saw God in water to drink and manna to eat. After he built a tabernacle in obedience to God, Moses said, "God, I want to see your glory."

You might say, "C'mon, Moses, enough is enough! I mean, you've really seen a lot!" And Moses would say, "But not enough." God took him up into the mountain and showed him a flaming finger that etched the law of God in the tablets of stone, and when Moses came down, it was not enough for him. It was never enough. He kept going back up. "I pray Thee," he said in Exodus 33:18, "show me Thy glory." This is the characteristic of a son of the kingdom. Always the hunger for more.

David was the man after God's own heart who walked in close communion with the Lord. He wrote Psalm 23. He had known God all his life. God had protected him and cared for him. Zeal for God's house had eaten him up. The pain that fell on God fell on him. He knew God intimately.

Yet, what did he say in Psalm 42:1-2? He cried out, "As the deer pants for the water brooks, so my soul pants for Thee, O God. My soul thirsts for God, for the living God." In Psalm 63:1 he says, "O God, Thou art my God." But he didn't stop there. "I shall seek Thee earnestly; my soul thirsts for Thee, my flesh yearns for Thee, in a dry and weary land where there is no water."

He's saying that the hunger and thirst never diminish. In a true son of the kingdom, this is the way of life.

The apostle Paul had three personal visions of Jesus Christ, beginning on the Damascus Road (Acts 9:3-9), then at Corinth (Acts 18:9-10), and then caught up into the third heaven to see things too wonderful to behold (2 Corinthians 12:1-4). Paul wrote theology and penned the great expressions of divine truth in the New Testament. What more could he want?

Yet the cry of his heart in Philippians 3:10 is, "That I may know Him, and the power of His resurrection and the fellowship of His sufferings." It's never enough. Sure, he knew the law. In verses 6-8 he says, in effect, "I knew the righteousness of the law, but I counted that as rubbish. I just want to know God."

J. N. Darby, the thoughtful man of God who was responsible for the early days of the Plymouth Brethren movement, said, "To be hungry is not enough. I must be really *starving* to know what is in God's heart toward me. When the prodigal son was hungry, he went to feed on the husks. But when he was starving, he went to his father." (Quoted in Lloyd-Jones, *Studies in the Sermon on the Mount,* 1:81.) That's the kind of desperation only God can satisfy.

Not until people hunger and thirst after righteousness do they seek the fulfillment that God can give. In Luke 1:53, the Bible says, "He has filled the hungry with good things; and sent away the rich empty-handed." (See also Psalm 107:9.) To hunger and thirst is intense, and it knows no end. I believe I hunger more for the righteousness of God now than I ever did, and I believe tomorrow that I'll hunger more for it than I did today.

What is it we are to hunger and thirst for?

Amos says that the people in the world pant after the dust of the earth (Amos 2:7). People are really after happiness, but the dusty earth is where they look for it. The number of amusements in our society always amazes me. Now, I'm not against Disneyland, Knott's Berry Farm, and all the rest. But our life is so full of amusements and entertainment possibilities. And we're like a man with a painful disease who just wants to be relieved of the pain and doesn't want to bother with the cause.

This has become true even in the church. Many Christians

are after some kind of an ecstasy. They want an experience, a spiritual feeling. People run to seminars and conferences and counselors trying to get some spiritual trip, but that is not what they are to seek. They try to find happiness, without facing the fact that happiness is a by-product of hungering and thirsting after righteousness. It is not in getting zapped with some holy high.

Righteousness, in the Greek *dikaiosuna*, or justification, means to be right with God. The only real happiness in life is to be right with God.

This points to two things: salvation and sanctification. Let's talk first about salvation. Somebody who hungers and thirsts after righteousness seeks salvation. He sees his sin, he sees his rebellion, he sees himself separated from a holy God. He is broken, mournful, meek, and he wants very much to restore himself to God. He wants forgiveness, and so he hungers and thirsts after the righteousness that comes in salvation. It is a desire to be free from self. It is a desire to be free from sin, its power, its presence, and its penalty.

Isaiah repeatedly equates righteousness with salvation. (See Isaiah 45:8; 46:12-13; 51:5; 56:1; 61:10.) You receive it at the moment of salvation. In fact, we can insert salvation as a substitute word in the Beatitude: "Blessed are those who hunger and thirst for *salvation*." Do you want to be happy? Hunger for salvation. Hunger to be saved. Hunger to have the blood of Christ cleanse your sin. Hunger to have the righteousness of Christ applied to you. When a man abandons all hope of saving himself and begins to hunger for a salvation that he can receive only at the hands of God, then he is going to know happiness.

This is where the Jews of Jesus' day were hung up. They were trying to gain salvation by their own works. They were saying, "We are filled up already with righteousness," but Jesus was saying, "Until you are flat on your back, hungering and thirsting for the true righteousness that you can't earn, you'll never know what it is to be happy."

Happiness belongs to the holy. Remember that in time of most urgent crisis and need, Paul said, "Rejoice." If you're unhappy, somewhere along the line you're unholy. Jesus was talking to Jews who thought they were righteous. To them, holiness was a conformity to rules. It was external. But it was not enough. That's why Jesus said, "Unless your righteousness surpasses that of the scribes and Pharisees, you shall not enter the kingdom" (Matthew 5:20). Their righteousness doesn't cut it. The Beatitudes took the external, stripped it away, and forced a look at the inside.

As I said, there's a second element: sanctification. We hunger and thirst for sanctification, an increasing holiness. I do not know how to express this as strongly as I feel it, but I hope there is in my life this hunger that never stops—the desire to be more and more like Christ. This is a mark of a Christian. We keep hungering and thirsting to desire more virtue, a greater purity. We never get to the place in which we think, "I've arrived." Such a thought is a most tragic attitude, both by unregenerate people who think they have saved themselves and by Christians who think they have arrived. (See Philippians 3:13-14.) Sons of the kingdom never stop hungering.

Paul says in Philippians 1:9, "And this I pray, that your love may abound still more and more." You're not done. No matter how much you love, you ought to love more. No matter how much you pray, you ought to pray more. No matter how much you obey, you ought to obey more. No matter how much you think like Christ, you ought to think like Christ more. Blessed are those who *continually* hunger and thirst.

It isn't that we're just seeking bits and pieces of righteousness. We are seeking the totality of righteousness, all the righteousness there is. To be like Christ. We are never satisfied. No matter how much righteousness we may have by God's grace, we don't have all there is, right? So, the hunger and thirst go on and we cry out, like David in Psalm

17:15, "I will be satisfied when I awake in this likeness [and I will not be satisfied until I do]."

So, it begins with salvation and it continues with sanctification, and we can never be satisfied with just a part of it. It also fascinates me that hungering and thirsting after righteousness, rather than *possessing* righteousness, is commended. The Jews would have said, "That's us. We all possess it."

Jesus blasted that idea. He said the people who think they've got it aren't blessed; the people who know they haven't got it, are. Just when you think you are righteous, you are the most desperate you have ever been. God blesses those who hunger and thirst so that they will always want more. Someone has called it a "thirst no earthly stream can satisfy, a hunger that must feed on Christ or die."

I call it divine discontent.

What is the result of this hungering and thirsting?

"They shall be filled" (KJV). *Filled* is a super word. It's used to describe foddering up an animal. It means to be absolutely satisfied. God wants to make us happy and satisfied. Satisfied with what? What are we hungry for? What are we thirsting for? Righteousness.

Isn't this a great paradox? You're satisfied but never satisfied. My wife makes a good lemon cream pie, a special kind. I'm always so satisfied when I eat that pie, but I always want more. I'm full, but I always want more because what I've already eaten makes me desire it. So it is with righteousness. We are filled, and the filling is so sweet and so rich and so full that we want more.

When we seek God's righteousness, He grants it. Psalm 107:9 says, "He has satisfied the thirsty soul, and the hungry soul He has filled with what is good." Psalm 34:10, "But they who seek the LORD shall not be in want of any good thing." Psalm 23, "I shall not want," and "My cup overflows." Jeremiah 31:14, " 'My people shall be satisfied with

My goodness,' declares the LORD."

In John 4:14 Jesus told the woman at the well, "Whoever drinks of the water that I shall give him shall never thirst." In John 6:35, He said, "I am the bread of life; he who comes to Me shall not hunger."

Jesus satisfies, and yet there is a blessed dissatisfaction that wants even more and will be satisfied only when we see Jesus Christ. A kingdom person has a consuming ambition, not for power or pleasure, not for possessions or praise, but for righteousness.

How do I know if I'm really thirsting and hungering after righteousness?

Are you satisfied with yourself? The Puritans, used to say, "He has the most need of righteousness who least wants it." Do you find yourself in Romans 7 all the time, saying, 'O wretched man that I am! Who shall deliver me from the body of this death?'? " Or are you so self-righteous that you think everybody else is wrong and you're right? If there is in you any sense of self-satisfaction, I wonder whether you know what it is to hunger and thirst after righteousness. Do you feel a constant pain of always falling short? That's a symptom of one who seeks God's way.

Does anything external satisfy you? Do you find that *things* have an influence on how you feel? Do you fill your appetite with the wrong stuff and then lose that appetite? A hunger for righteousness will be satisfied with nothing else.

Do you have a great appetite for the Word of God? The rules, the obedience of which brings about righteousness, are in His Word. Jeremiah said, "Thy words were found and I ate them" (Jeremiah 15:16). If you're hungering and thirsting after righteousness, you will have such an appetite for the Word that you will devour it. If you're not hungering and thirsting after righteousness, maybe you are a kingdom child who's being sinful. Or maybe you're not a child of the kingdom at all. Either way, there is a forfeiting of happiness.

Are the things of God sweet to you? Proverbs 27:7 says, "To a famished man any bitter thing is sweet." I can recognize somebody who is seeking righteousness, because when God brings devastation into his life, he is filled and satisfied. He receives it of God, even though it's painful. Some people can rejoice only when good things happen. When tough things happen, they don't like it. They are not hungering and thirsting; they are merely chasing happiness.

Thomas Watson says, "The one who hungers and thirsts after righteousness can feed on the myrrh of the gospel as well as the honey." (Watson, *The Beatitudes*, p. 128.) I can tell you from personal experience, trials can be as sweet as the good times because God is in them and is working His purposes, making us more righteous.

Is your hunger and thirst unconditional? Remember the rich young ruler who told Jesus Christ that he wanted to know how to enter the kingdom, but he wasn't willing to give up his possessions? His hunger was conditional, and he was never filled. What about you? Do you say, "I want Christ and my sin. Christ and my pride. Christ and my illicit relationship. Christ and my cheating. Christ and my lying. Christ and my covetousness. Christ and my materialism. Christ and, Christ and. . ."?

A hungry man does not want food and a new suit. A thirsty man does not want water and a new pair of shoes. They just want food and water. Psalm 119:20 says, "My soul is crushed with longing after Thine ordinances at all times."

How did you do on the test? Isaiah 26:9 says, "At night my soul longs for Thee, indeed, my spirit within me seeks Thee diligently." David thirsted for God diligently and early. The wise virgins had their oil before the bridegroom came. There are some people who are going to thirst too late, and they are going to be like the rich man in Luke 16:24.

They might be heard saying, "Oh, send someone who can dip the tip of his finger in the water and cool my tongue, for I am tormented in this flame!" Such is the thirst when there can be no remedy.

Thirst now, and be filled.

7

"Happy Are the Merciful. . ."

Matthew 5:7

"Blessed are the merciful, for they shall receive mercy."

The religion Jesus faced in His day was shallow, superficial, external and very much ritualistic. The Jewish leaders thought they were secure and that they would surely be inhabiters of the kingdom. They thought they would be leaders in Messiah's rule.

But our Lord said to those people, "For you are like whitewashed tombs which on the outside appear beautiful, but inside they are full of dead men's bones and all uncleanness" (Matthew 23:27). Back in Matthew 3:7-12, when John the Baptist arrived on the scene and saw many of the Pharisees and Sadducees come for baptism, John said to them: "You brood of vipers, who warned you to flee from the wrath to come? Therefore bring forth fruit in keeping with your repentance; and do not suppose that you can say to yourselves, 'We have Abraham for our father'" (Matthew 3:7-9). In other words, don't count on your racial identity to save you.

> For I say to you, that God is able from these stones to raise up children to Abraham. And the axe is already

laid at the root of the trees; every tree therefore that
does not bear good fruit is cut down and thrown into
the fire. As for me, I baptize you in water for repentance, but He who is coming after me is mightier than I,
and I am not even fit to remove His sandals; He Himself
will baptize you with the Holy Spirit and fire. And His
winnowing fork is in His hand, and He will thoroughly
clean His threshing floor; and He will gather His wheat
into the barn, but He will burn up the chaff with un-
quenchable fire [vv. 9-12].

John the Baptist was speaking of a tremendous judgment
that would come on those who had nothing more than an
external religion. The axe was falling, the fire was beginning.

Jesus confronts this external, self-righteous, selfish crowd
and says, "What really matters is on the inside." He by-
passed all the supposed credits they had mounted to their
own cause and went straight to the heart of the matter.
Christ always puts the emphasis on the inside. He is not
unconcerned with outward action, but only as it is produced
by proper motivation.

Righteousness on the inside will produce the fruit of right
action. But you can falsify action without reality, and that's
legalism. What Jesus wants is action that springs from right
character.

The sixth and seventh chapters of Matthew deal with action: things we do or say or think. The premise on which the
whole Sermon is built is the heart attitude. Martyn Lloyd-
Jones has well put it, "A Christian *is* something before he
does something." (Lloyd-Jones, *Studies in the Sermon on the
Mount,* 1:96.)

To be a child of the king, a subject of the kingdom, is first
to possess a certain kind of character, a character of brokenness, a mourning over sin, meekness, a hunger and thirst
for righteousness, mercifulness, purity of heart, a
peacemaking quality. We are not meant to control our Chris-

tianity. Our Christianity is meant to control us.

Living as a Christian means there is to be no veneer, no facade. Christianity is something that happens to us at the very center of our being, and from there it flows out to the activities of life. God has never been interested in only the blood of bulls and goats. He has never been interested in any superficial spiritual activity unless the heart is right. (See Amos 5:21-24.)

So Jesus confronted a crowd of externalists with some devastating comments. In the first Beatitude He says, "What you need to do is be spiritually bankrupt. You need to recognize that you are destitute and debauched beggars who have nothing good to bring to God and that your only hope is to see your condition and cower in the darkness and reach out as one who can't do anything for himself. You must not be satisfied with your self-righteousness. You must weep great tears for your sinfulness. Further, you must not be proud because you have kept certain laws. You must be meek before a holy God. You must realize that you are starving for a lack of righteousness."

The first four Beatitudes were entirely inner principles, dealing with how you see yourself before God. This fifth Beatitude, while also being an inner attitude, begins to reach out and touch others. This is the fruit of the other four. When we are broken as beggars in our spirit, when we are mournful and meek and hungering and thirsting after righteousness, being merciful to others will be the result.

The first four Beatitudes line up with the last four. The first four are inner attitudes and the last four are the things the attitudes manifest.

When we have poverty of spirit and we realize that we are nothing but beggars, we will be willing to give to another beggar, so we will be merciful.

When we mourn over our sin, we wash our hearts pure with the tears of penitence, and we will be pure in heart.

When we are meek, we will be peacemakers, because

meekness makes peace.

And when we are hungering and thirsting for righteousness, we will be willing to be persecuted for righteousness's sake

Now, let's look at what it means to be merciful. Jesus' simple statement here is so profound and so broad in its implications that I hardly know where to begin. I have the feeling that there is no way I could begin to cover it all, even if I took the space of this entire book just for verse 7. But let's take a shot at it.

The significance of mercy

What does it mean to be merciful? The Jews of that day hardly knew. They were as merciless as the Romans. They were proud, egotistical, self-righteous, and condemning. What Jesus was saying really touched them where they lived.

People often want to take this Beatitude in a humanistic way. They say, "Well, if you're good to everybody else, everybody else will be good to you." Even the Talmud recognizes some sort of magnanimous human virtue in mercy when it quotes Gamaliel: "Whenever thou hast mercy, God will have mercy on thee, and if thou hast not mercy, neither will God have mercy on thee."

It seems built into human thinking that if you're good to everybody, they'll return the kindness. Even people who look at it theologically, as Gamaliel did, think, "Well, if I do this for God, God's going to do that for me."

One writer paraphrased this Beatitude this way: "This is the great truth of life, if people see us care, they will care." But it's not that simple. If you bring God into it, there is certain reciprocation. If we truly honor God, God will care for us, as Gamaliel indicated. But the world does not work that way, believe me. In fact, the Roman world did not know the meaning of mercy, no matter what good was done.

A Roman philosopher said mercy was "the disease of the soul," a sign of weakness. The Romans glorified justice and courage and discipline and power; they looked down on mercy. When a child was born into the Roman world the father had the right of *patria potestas.* If he wanted the new-born to live, he held his thumb up. If he wanted the child to die, he held it down and the child was immediately drowned.

If a Roman citizen didn't want his slave any more, he could kill and bury him, and there would be no legal recourse against the citizen. He could also kill his wife if he chose. So if you were talking to people under Roman power, you could not try to tell them that mercy begets mercy on the human level. It just wouldn't cut it.

It's wishful thinking in our selfish, grabbing, competitive society, too. In our day, we would more likely say, "Be merciful to someone and he'll step on your neck!"

The best illustration that this is no valid human platitude is our Lord Jesus Christ Himself. He was the most merciful human being who ever lived. He reached out to the sick and healed them. He reached out to the crippled and gave them legs to walk. He healed the eyes of the blind, the ears of the deaf, and the mouths of the dumb. He found prostitutes and tax collectors and those that were debauched and drunken, and He drew them into the circle of His love and redeemed them and set them on their feet.

He took the lonely and made them feel loved. He took little children and gathered them into His arms and loved them. Never was there a person on the face of the earth with the mercy of this One. Once a funeral procession came by and He saw a mother weeping because her son was dead. She was already a widow, and now she had no child to care for her. Who would care? Jesus stopped the funeral procession, put His hand on the casket, and raised the child from the dead. He cared.

In John 8 he forgave a woman taken in adultery. What

mercy! When the scribes and Pharisees saw Him eat with the tax collectors and the sinners in Mark 2:16, they asked His disciples, "Why is He eating and drinking with tax-gatherers and sinners?" He ran around with the riff-raff!

He was the most merciful human being who ever lived, and they screamed for His blood. If mercy carried its own reward, they would not have nailed Him to a cross and spit in His face and cursed Him. From the people to whom He gave mercy he received no mercy at all.

Two merciless systems, Roman and Judaic, united to kill Him. No, mercy as talked about here is not some human virtue that brings its own reward. That is not the idea.

Then what does the Lord mean? Simply this: You be merciful to others, and *God* will be merciful to you. God is the subject of the second phrase.

The word itself, *merciful*, is from the Greek *eliamosuna*, from which we get the word *eleemosynary*, which means *benefactory*. The word is used in this form only one other time in the New Testament. The other is in Hebrews 2:17, "Therefore, He had to be made like His brethren in all things, that He might become a *merciful* and faithful high priest." Christ is the great illustration of mercy. He is the High Priest who intercedes for us, and it is from Him that mercy comes.

The verb form is very common in Scripture. In Matthew 6:3 it is used concerning almsgiving. The Hebrew synonym would be *chesed*, which means "to have mercy on, to succor the afflicted, to give help to the wretched, and to rescue the miserable." Anything you do that is of benefit to someone in need is mercy.

We think of mercy so much in terms of forgiveness in salvation, but it is really a much broader term. It goes beyond compassion. It goes beyond sympathy. It means sympathy and compassion in action toward anyone in need. When our Lord talks about it here, the real *eliamosuna* is not the weak sympathy that carnal selfishness feels but never does anything about. It is not that false mercy that indulges its own flesh in salving of conscience by giving tokenism. It is not the silent, passive pity that never seems to help in a tangible way. It is genuine compassion with a pure, unselfish motive that reaches out to help.

In other words, Jesus was saying to them, "The people in my kingdom aren't takers—they're givers. The people in my kingdom aren't the ones who set themselves above everybody—they're the people who stoop to help."

Jesus told them a story about a man who would not give even the necessary funds to care for his father and mother because he said, "I already devoted it to God in a religious act, and I dare not break my vow." Jesus said, "You are in deep trouble. You have exchanged the commandment of God to honor your father and mother for a tradition that you've invented yourself." (See Matthew 15:1-9.)

The Jews were good at that! They were merciless even to their own parents.

Mercy is seeing a man without food and giving him food. Mercy is seeing a person begging for love and giving him love. Mercy is seeing someone lonely and giving him company. Mercy is *meeting* the need, not just feeling it.

Our understanding can be aided by a brief discussion about mercy in relation to similar words in Scripture. This may appear complicated, but stay with me and I think you will be as fascinated as I was to discover these truths.

Titus 3:5 tells us that "He saved us . . . according to His mercy." In Ephesians 2:4-9 we learn that God has saved us "being rich in mercy." It is God's mercy that allows Him to redeem us. So mercy is behind forgiveness. Mercy and forgiveness belong together.

In Daniel 9:9 (KJV) it says, "To the Lord our God belong mercies and forgivenesses." Psalm 130:1-7 (KJV) also beautifully links mercy and forgiveness:

> Out of the depths have I cried unto Thee, O LORD. Lord, hear my voice: let thine ears be attentive to the voice of

my supplications. If thou, LORD, shouldest mark iniquities, O Lord, who shall stand? But there is forgiveness with thee, that thou mayest be feared. I wait for the
LORD, my soul doth wait, and in his word do I hope. My
soul waiteth for the Lord more than they that watch for
the morning: I say, more than they that watch for the
morning. Let Israel hope in the LORD: for with the LORD
there is mercy.

Here's an individual confessing sin, seeking forgiveness,
and knowing that forgiveness comes from the fountain of
mercy. We cannot think of mercy without its expression in
forgiveness, and we cannot think of forgiveness without its
source, mercy. *But,* forgiveness is not the only expression of
mercy. We cannot narrow mercy.

Mercy is infinitely bigger than just forgiveness. Psalm
119:64 (KJV) says, "The earth, O LORD, is full of thy mercy."
Genesis 32:10 (KJV), "I am not worthy of the least of all the
mercies." Second Samuel 24:14, "For His mercies are great."
Nehemiah 9:19 (KJV), "Thy manifold mercies." Psalm 69:13
(KJV), "The multitude of Thy mercy." Forgiveness is an act
of mercy, yes, but there are many other ways I can be merciful.

In Lamentations, maybe the most beautiful of all the
mercy passages, it says this: "It is of the LORD'S mercies that
we are not consumed, because his compassions fail not.
They are new every morning: great is thy faithfulness"
(3:22-23, KJV).

What about mercy and love? How do they compare? We
said that forgiveness flows out of mercy. What does mercy
flow out of? Love. Why has God been merciful? "But God,
being rich in mercy, because of His great love with which
He loved us" (Ephesians 2:4). Do you see the sequence? God
loves and love is merciful, and mercy is forgiving, among
many other things.

But love is bigger than mercy. Mercy is bigger than forgiveness and love is bigger than mercy, because love can do

a lot more things than just show mercy. Mercy presupposes a problem. Love can act when there isn't a problem.

For example, the Father loves the Son, and the Son does not need mercy. The Father loves the angels and the angels love the Father and neither of them need mercy. Mercy is the physician; love is the friend. Love acts out of affection; mercy acts out of need. Love is constant; mercy is reserved for times of trouble. There is no mercy without love. See how God's great love funnels down to our need under the category of mercy?

There's a whole other category too. When we're righteous and don't need mercy, He still loves. He shall love us throughout eternity when we do not need mercy anymore. But in this life, love funnels down to us through mercy, and mercy narrows down to that one thought of forgiveness.

What about mercy and grace? You are about to get a real theological exercise, so hang on. The term *mercy* and all its derivatives always presuppose problems. It deals with the pain and the misery and distress. But grace deals with the sin itself. Mercy deals with the symptoms; grace deals with the problems. Mercy offers relief from punishment; grace offers pardon for the crime. First comes grace. Grace removes the sin. Then mercy eliminates the punishment.

In the story of the Good Samaritan, mercy relieves the suffering. Grace rents him a room. Mercy deals with the negative and grace puts it in the positive. Mercy takes away the pain; grace gives a better condition. Mercy says, "No hell." Grace says, "Heaven." Mercy says, "I pity you." Grace says, "I pardon you." So mercy and grace are two sides of the same marvelous coin. God offers both.

What about mercy and justice? People say, "Well, if God is a God of justice, how can He be merciful?" If you look at it that way, if God's a just, holy, righteous God, can He negate justice? Can He say, "I know you're a sinner, and I know you've done awful things, but I have so much mercy, I'm going to forgive you." Can He do that? Yes, He can. Why?

Because He came into the world in human form and died on the cross and bore in His own body our sins.

He paid the price for all our sin. At the cross, when Jesus died, justice was satisfied. God said there would be no forgiveness without the shedding of blood. God said there had to be a perfect sacrifice to bear the sins of the world. Jesus was that. Justice was satisfied. Mercy does no violation to justice.

When I talk about the mercy of God, I do not speak of some foolish sentimentality that excuses sin. Too much of that is already going on, even in the church. The only time God ever extended mercy was when somebody paid the price for the sin involved. There is a false, foolish, sentimental mercy that wants simply to cancel out justice and does not want to make people pay for anything. King Saul spared King Agag (1 Samuel 15). That violated God's holiness. David, in a counterfeit mercy shown to Absalom, let him off easy and sowed the seeds of rebellion in his heart (2 Samuel 13). Don't ever forget it. Psalm 85:10 (KJV) says, "Mercy and truth are met together."

God will never violate the truth of His justice and His holiness to be merciful. He will be merciful, but only when justice has been done. If Absalom had repented and had accepted the truth of God, then the mercy would have been real. But it was not, because he never acquiesced.

There are people in the church who sin and never really deal with the evil. Yet they want mercy. Look at James 2, starting with verse 10: "For whoever keeps the whole law and yet stumbles in one point, he has become guilty of all. For He who said, 'Do not commit adultery,' also said, 'Do not commit murder.' Now if you do not commit adultery, but do commit murder, you have become a transgressor of the law. So speak and so act, as those who are to be judged by the law of liberty. For judgment will be merciless to one who has shown no mercy."

There will be a merciless judgment on people who do not

accept the truth, the sacrifice of Christ. We are not talking about sentimentality. If you sin your life away and never acknowledge Jesus Christ, God offers no promise to be merciful to you or to accept you. You will have judgment without mercy.

So mercy is special. It is more than forgiveness. It is less than love. It is different from grace. And it is one with justice. The merciful one not only hears the insults of evil men, but his heart also reaches out to them in compassion. The merciful one is sympathetic. He is forgiving. He is gracious and loving. He is not so sentimental that he will allow sin to go unpunished or unconfronted just because somebody is sort of sad or tragic.

Psalm 37:21 (KJV) says this: "The wicked borroweth and payeth not again: but the righteous sheweth mercy." If my son comes to me and says, "Dad, I did something wrong, and I'm sorry," I'll be merciful. But I've told my children since they were little, "If I find out that you haven't told me the truth or you haven't admitted something you've done, there won't be mercy. There'll be punishment."

It was mercy in Abraham after he had been wronged by his nephew Lot that caused him to go and secure Lot's deliverance.

It was mercy in Joseph after being treated so badly by his brothers that caused him to accept them and meet their needs.

It was mercy in Moses, after Miriam had rebelled against him, and the Lord had given her leprosy, that made him cry, "Oh God, heal her, I pray!" (Numbers 12:13).

It was mercy in David that twice caused him to spare the life of Saul. (See 1 Samuel 24 and 26.)

In Psalm 109:14-15 we read about the person without mercy. "Let the iniquity of his fathers be remembered before the LORD, and do not let the sin of his mother be blotted out. Let them be before the LORD continually, that He may cut off the memory of them from the earth." Why? Oh, God, why would You be so judgmental? Why so condemning? "Because he did not remember to show lovingkindness [mercy], but persecuted the afflicted and needy man, and the despondent in heart, to put them to death" (v. 16).

The merciful are those who reach out, not those who grasp and take. God help us to be able somehow to overrule the inundation of a corrupt society and hear the voice of our God who tells us to give everything we have.

If somebody offends us, we should be merciful. Be compassionate. Be benevolent. Be sympathetic. If somebody makes a mistake or a misjudgment or fails to pay a debt or return something they've borrowed, be merciful. We must live the character of the kingdom.

In Proverbs 11:17 it says, "The merciful man does himself good, but the cruel man does himself harm." Do you want to be really miserable? Be merciless. Do you want to be happy? Be merciful. Proberbs 12:10 (KJV): "The righteous man regardeth the life of his beast but the tender mercies of the wicked are cruel." Righteous people are merciful even to animals. The wicked are cruel to everything.

Do you want to read the characteristics of a godless society? Romans 1:29-31 says, "Being filled with all unrighteousness, wickedness, greed, malice; full of envy, murder, strife, deceit, malice; they are gossips, slanderers, haters of God, insolent, arrogant, boastful, inventors of evil, disobedient to parents, without understanding, untrustworthy, unloving, unmerciful."

Does this mean the climax the of the whole thing is being unmerciful? It appears so.

For those of us who have received mercy, how could we be anything but merciful? What did we deserve? If we needed mercy so desperately from God, how can we demand to be cruel to somebody? And that takes us to our next point.

The source of mercy

God is the source of mercy, but only for the people moving through the four preceding Beatitudes. Mercy is not a normal human attribute. Now and then someone might return a kindness, but that is not the norm. The only way to be merciful persons is to have within us the God-given mercy. And the only way to have that is to have the righteousness of God that comes through Christ. That's what Jesus is saying. If we come by this Beatitude path to the place of hungering and thirsting for righteousness, to be filled by God, we will know mercy.

People want the blessing, but they do not want the belonging. They are like Balaam, the false prophet, who said, "Let me die the death of the upright" (Numbers 23:10). A Puritan commentator said, "Balaam wanted to die like the righteous all right, he just didn't want to live like the righteous." The only people who have mercy are the people who have come with a broken and beggarly spirit before a holy God and sought His righteousness.

In Psalm 103:11 (KJV) the psalmist says, "As the heaven is high above the earth, so great is his mercy toward them that fear him." We fear God, we come to Christ, and God gives us His mercy. Thus, the Lord says in Luke 6:36, "Be merciful, just as your Father is merciful." Nothing can rival the cross for mercy, for it fulfilled Christ's role as a merciful high priest (Hebrews 2:17). Dr. Donald Grey Barnhouse put it this way:

> When Jesus Christ died on the cross, all the work of God for man's salvation passed out of the realm of prophecy and became historical fact. God has now had mercy upon us. For anyone to pray, 'God have mercy on me' is the equivalent of asking Him to repeat the sacrifice of Christ. All the mercy that God ever will have on man He has already had, when Christ died. That is the totality of mercy. There couldn't be any more. And God can now act toward us in grace because He has already had

all mercy on us. The fountain is now opened, and flow-
ing, and flows freely. [Donald Grey Barnhouse, *God's
Discipline* (Grand Rapids: Eerdmans), p. 4.]

The substance of mercy

What does it mean to be merciful? Matthew 5-6, Romans
15, 2 Corinthians 1, Galatians 6, Ephesians 4, Colossians 3,
along with countless other passages, will all answer this
question for you for they call us to be merciful. How can you
be merciful?

1. Physically.

By giving a poor man money, a hungry man food, a naked
man clothes, a bedless man a bed. The Old Testament is
loaded with ways that we can show mercy. Mercy never
holds a grudge, never retaliates, never takes vengeance,
never flaunts somebody's weakness, never makes something of someone's failure, never recites a sin. St. Augustine
was so merciful to others that he invited people who had no
place to eat to come to his big, beautiful dining room table.
On the top of the table it is said he had engraved: "Whoever
loves another's name to blast, this table's not for him, so let
him fast." (Watson, *The Beatitudes*, p. 149.)

The vindictive, self-righteous, defensive person who pro-
tects only himself is like the priest and the Levite who went
on the other side of the road from the helpless man the Good
Samaritan aided.

2. Spiritually.

Pity. St. Augustine said, "If I weep for the body from
which the soul is departed, should I not weep for the soul
from which God is departed?" (Quoted in Watson, *The
Beatitudes*, p. 144.) We cry a lot of tears over dead bodies.
What do we do when it comes to souls? If I as a Christian
had no righteousness but was poor in spirit. If I stood
mourning over my sin in a beggarly and hopeless condem-
nation. If I was wretched and doomed and meek. If I
hungered and thirsted for what I had to have but could not

produce. If, after all that, I was given mercy and pity from God's great heart but did not let that same mercy flow to others—what kind of consistency would that be?

I hear Stephen saying as they cast the stones and crushed out his life, "Lord, do not hold this sin against them!" (Acts 7:60). He was pitying their souls. You and I must look at the lost with pity, not lording it over them or thinking ourselves better.

Prodding. Second Timothy 2:25 tells us, "With gentleness correcting those who are in opposition, if perhaps God may grant them repentance leading to the knowledge of the truth." Prodding means to confront people about their sin in order that God might give them forgiveness. They have got to hear the gospel.

Titus 1:13 says, "Reprove them severely that they may be sound in the faith." I can care for the soul of a sinner by rebuking him to his face. Such an act is not unloving. In Jude 23 it says that there are some people whom you have to save with fear, "snatching them out of the fire." That's not hatred or cruelty; that's love.

Mercy prods. There has to be the confrontation about sin before there can ever be the realization of sinfulness.

Pray. Prayer for the souls of those without God is an act of mercy. Do we pray for the lost? Do we pray for our neighbors? Do we pray for Christians who are walking in disobedience? Our prayer is an act of mercy, for it releases God's blessing.

Preaching. I believe preaching the gospel is the most necessary and merciful thing you can do for the lost soul.

So, we can be merciful to a person's soul by pity, by prodding, by prayer, and by preaching.

The sequel to mercy

The sequel to mercy is obtaining mercy. What a beautiful thing. Do you see the cycle? God gives us mercy, we are merciful, and God gives us more mercy. Second Samuel

22:26 says the same thing, that it is the merciful who receive mercy. James 2:13 says it negatively, "For judgment will be merciless to one who has shown no mercy."

It's there in Psalm 18 and Proverbs 14. But now we must be warned of something, and this is critical.

Some people think being merciful is how we get saved. This is the error of the Roman Catholic Church, that God is satisfied and gives mercy when we do merciful deeds. That view spawned monasteries and nunneries and everything related to them. But this is not the way to earn salvation. We do not get mercy for merit. Mercy can apply only where there is no merit, or it is not mercy.

The one who has received mercy will be merciful. The one who has received forgiveness will be forgiving. If you are a merciful person, you give evidence of being God's child; so every time you sin, God forgives. Every time you have a need, He meets it. He takes care of you. He just pours mercy upon mercy upon mercy to those who *show* mercy, because they have received it from the merciful God.

Are you merciful?

8
"Happy Are the Holy. . ."

Matthew 5:8

Some truths in the Bible you feel you can handle; some you feel you can get a grip on and transmit. Then there are those things that seem like bottomless pits, wells whose depths are immeasurable, truths the breadths of which are impossible to encompass. "Blessed are the pure in heart, for they shall see God," is one of those.

To attempt to deal with such an incredible statement in one brief chapter is almost an insult to God and to the power and depth and insight of His Word. This is one of the greatest utterances in all the Bible. It stretches over everything else revealed in Scripture. The theme of purity of heart being necessary to see God is vast and infinite and draws in almost every biblical thread.

There's no way to uncover all that's available, but I've asked the Lord to help me at least to focus on a central lesson that will be rich and meaningful. I find that the best way to approach something like this is to ask questions of the verses.

What is the context for these words historically and chronologically within the Beatitudes?

To me, the statement about purity of heart is so crucial that it doesn't seem right to see it as just sort of stuck in there indiscriminately, as it often appears at first glance. I wondered why it does not have a more strategic place, perhaps at the beginning or the end of the sermon. So, we shall discuss the context, but first from a historical sense.

We have dealt with the political situation in Israel at the time of Christ in great detail, so I want to focus now on their spiritual condition. This, of course, is the issue with which He deals predominantly in the Sermon on the Mount. Verse 8 has at its heart a spiritual reality.

Israel was burdened by an oppressive, authoritative character on the part of the Pharisees. They were the dominant influence and force on Israel at that time. (A legalistic system draws such absolute boundaries around what is spiritually acceptable that, by virtue of its definitive character, it tends to oppress and reign wherever it exists.)

The Pharisees had misinterpreted the law of Moses. They had invented new laws so that, if they couldn't keep God's laws, they could pacify their consciences by keeping traditions. They formed a relentless and imposingly rigid legalistic system on the people, and it was impossible to perform it. In fact, the leaders themselves had decided that if one could keep just a few of the laws, God would understand. Then they couldn't even do that, so they agreed that if one could just find one law and keep it, God would understand. (Hence the question of the lawyer in Matthew 22:36.)

So the mass of people in Israel were frustrated by a legal system they could not keep, and it produced in them tremendous guilt and anxiety. Yet, here was a people committed to the reality of God and to the fact that He had revealed Himself in laws. I believe this is one of the things that contributed so dramatically to the power of John the Baptist's ministry.

He had a ready audience because people were looking for someplace to relieve their burden of sin. Multitudes flocked to hear him preach in the wilderness; even the Pharisees and Sadducees would show up. The people's hearts were aching for a sense of forgiveness, the reality of salvation, a sense of tranquility for their troubled souls.

They were crying for a savior, a redeemer—one who would not impose more rules on them, but one who would forgive them for the ones they had always broken. They knew that God, long before, had promised such a redeemer. And they knew the word of Isaiah well enough to know that there would come one who would forgive their sin, do away with their iniquity, right their wrongs. There would come one to find the remnant of honest and truly motivated people, the people who really worshiped God.

They knew the word of Ezekiel that some day God was going to come and sprinkle them with water, and they would be clean. God was going to take out the stony heart and put in a heart of flesh. God was going to wash them of their iniquities, purge them from their sins.

They knew the testimony of David, who knew what it was to have that sense of forgiveness, who knew what it was to cry, "How blessed is the man to whom the LORD does not impute iniquity" (Psalm 32:2). They knew it, but so many had never experienced it.

So, here they were, under this tremendous burden of oppression. When John the Baptist announced a Messiah, a Redeemer, a Savior, no wonder they came out. When he said, "Repent, for the kingdom of heaven is at hand" (Matthew 3:2), they couldn't get there fast enough to unload the burden and seek the forgiveness. A further reason I believe that is so is because that seemed to be the longing in the hearts of the people as they met Jesus.

For example, think of Nicodemus in John 3. There was a Pharisee, but a pretty honest guy (I believe his integrity drew him to Christ). He knew he was in real trouble if what Jesus said was true. In the Greek of verse 1, an emphatic is used to describe him. This man was *the* teacher, *the* ruler of the Jews, top man in terms of recitation of divine principles.

But his heart was full of anxiety. He came to Jesus and said, "Rabbi, we know that You have come from God as a teacher; for no man can do these signs that You do unless God is with him" (John 3:2). That's a tremendous insight into what was on Nicodemus's mind. He had found somebody from God. In his heart was this huge question: "What do I have to do to be righteous, to get into Your kingdom, to be a child of God, to be redeemed?"

Nicodemus never even asked the question, of course. He didn't get a chance. Jesus read his mind. Verse 3 says, "Jesus answered." Isn't that great? Sometimes you don't even need to ask the question. He knows. He just gives the answer. Jesus answered the question in Nicodemus's heart and said, "Truly, truly, I say to you, unless one is born again, he cannot see the kingdom of God."

Nicodemus had looked at his life and decided, "I know I'm a Pharisee, and I'm trying to keep the law, and I'm a ruler in the land, a teacher of the law, but I'm not sure this is enough." He was honest enough to admit his sinfulness. As one who had tried to keep the law, he had failed miserably.

What was on Nicodemus's heart, I believe, was on the hearts of many of the Jews, though Nicodemus may have been in a minute minority among the leaders.

Jesus had miraculously fed five thousand people (John 6), "They said therefore to Him, 'What shall we do, that we may work the works of God?' Jesus answered and said to them, 'This is the work of God, that you believe in Him whom He has sent' " (John 6:28-29).

What were they really saying? The same thing as Nicodemus. "We know the whole legal system. We know the whole ritualistic routine. We've got all the ceremonies down. What do we do to know the reality of the work of God?"

They wanted something real. They wanted to know how you really get into the kingdom, because if you got in by keeping the law, nobody would be in the kingdom, and they knew it.

Look at Luke 10:25: "And behold, a certain lawyer stood up and put Him to the test, saying, 'Teacher, what shall I do to inherit eternal life?' " It's the same question. That's what the multitude wants to know. That's what Nicodemus wants to know. What's the standard? How do you get relief from guilt and anxiety and frustration that comes when you are faced with a legal system to please God, and you know you cannot keep it?

This was the perfect time for Jesus to come, because He was the answer. You see, God is a holy God, absolutely righteous. In Him there is no sin. God offers salvation to sinful man, and sinful man says to himself, "How can a holy God give salvation to a sinful man?" An honest, devout Jew would say, "How can I ever enter God's kingdom when I can't keep God's laws?"

That poses the question that Jesus answers in the Beatitudes. That was the question most in the minds of the people sitting on that Galilean hillside as our Lord spoke in Matthew 5. Remember that He had gone all around Galilee teaching in the synagogues, preaching the gospel of the kingdom, healing all manner of diseases, and that His fame spread everywhere. The crowds had heard about Him. They had seen Him, heard His teaching, were aware of His miracles. And they had this one great question.

More than any other single Beatitude, this one gives the answer. "Blessed are the pure in heart, for they [*autoi*, they and they alone] shall see God." It is not those who observe the external washings. It is not those who go through the ceremonies. It is not those who have the religion of human achievement.

Man tends to measure himself by his fellow man. Second Corinthians 11 talks about false apostles who measure themselves by themselves. The Pharisees were good at that. Whenever you desire to test your character or morality or ethics or goodness, you just find somebody worse, and you're okay.

The Pharisee would pray like this, "God, I thank Thee that I am not like other people . . . even like this tax-gatherer" (Luke 18:11). His standard was lower than himself. The fallacy of that, of course, is that if everybody keeps basing his own evaluation on one person lower, the whole thing spirals down until the ultimate standard is the most rotten person alive.

When God set a standard for acceptable behavior, He did not say you had to be better than a Publican or an immoral man. He said, "If you want to see God, you have to be pure." In the sermon itself, in Matthew 5:48, He said, "Therefore you are to be perfect, as your heavenly Father is perfect." That's the standard of the absolute, holy, righteous, and only God of the universe.

Who will enter the kingdom? Who will go to heaven? Who is fit to enter God's presence? Who is saved? Who will ever have a vision of God? Who will ever enter into bliss? Who will know blessedness? Who will know true happiness? Only those who are pure in their hearts.

The Pharisees used to get uptight if they did not have certain washings of the hands and pots and pans, and they were great for tithing their mint and cummin and dill. They were sure they gave ten percent of some little, tiny herbal leaf, but they paid no attention to love and truth and mercy. Jesus told them, "For you are like whitewashed tombs which on the outside appear beautiful, but inside they are full of dead men's bones and all uncleanness" (Matthew 23:27). The Lord shreds that whole cloak of hypocrisy in one statement.

Now, if this is such a high point, such a key Beatitude, why does it come here in the list? Well, every one of these Beatitudes is critical. You cannot remove any of them. They flow in a beautiful, magnificent sequence, in perfect order according to the mind of God. It is not that the first or the last or the middle is more important. They are equally important. They are all part of the same great reality.

A kingdom person is one who fulfills all of these descriptions. You cannot pick and choose. Once you have come to the beginning and are poor in spirit, the rest flows out in a wonderful working of the Spirit of God. The first seven Beatitudes fit a beautiful pattern. The first three lead up to the fourth, to hunger and thirst after righteousness, which seems to be a kind of apex. You begin with a beggarly spirit, and out of that comes a mourning over sin. When you see yourself as a total sinner, you become humble and meek before God. At that point you cry out for righteousness. Then God acts and you find His mercy, purity of heart, and the gift of peacemaking. So these last three Beatitudes flow out of the fourth, after the first three lead up to it.

But did you notice something even more intricate? The first and the fifth, the second and the sixth, and the third and the seventh seem to fit together. It is the poor in spirit (first), who realize that they are nothing but beggars, who are going to reach out in mercy to others (fifth). Those who mourn over their sin (second) are going to know the purity of heart (sixth). Finally, there are the meek (third) who are the peacemakers (seventh).

The beautiful weaving together of these Beatitudes shows how the mind of God works. This one is in the right place historically and chronologically.

There are only two kinds of religion in the world. Only two. One is the religion of human achievement, which comes under every brand imaginable but is all from the same base, namely, you earn your own way. The other is the religion of divine accomplishment that says, "I can't do it. God did it in Christ."

Take your pick. Human achievement is Satan's lie. In every crowd you have people who are going to make it on their own; they are going to try to earn their way to heaven and get there on their own energy, power, and resources. They were in that crowd that day, and the Lord Jesus stripped them bare. "Sorry, folks. You don't qualify to see God. You'll never be in My kingdom. It is for the pure in heart."

Those people had no excuse. They must have known the Psalms. "Behold, Thou dost desire truth in the innermost being" (Psalm 51:6). The psalmist taught the same reality in Psalm 24:1-5:

> The earth is the LORD'S and all it contains, the world, and those who dwell in it. For He has founded it upon the seas, and established it upon the rivers. Who may ascend into the hill of the LORD? Who may stand in His holy place? He who has clean hands and a pure heart, who has not lifted up his soul to falsehood, and has not sworn deceitfully. He shall receive a blessing from the LORD and righteousness from the God of his salvation.

Who enters the kingdom? Jesus condenses Psalm 24 into this Beatitude. If the Jews had recalled the words of the beloved prophet Isaiah, whom they extolled so wonderfully, they would have known. It says in Isaiah 59:1, "Behold, the Lord's hand is not so short that it cannot save." If you are not saved it is not because God's arm cannot reach you.

> But your iniquities have made a separation between you and your God, and your sins have hidden His face from you, so that he does not hear. For your hands are defiled with blood, and your fingers with iniquity; your lips have spoken falsehood, your tongue mutters wickedness. No one sues righteously and no one pleads honestly. They trust in confusion, and speak lies; they conceive mischief, and bring forth iniquity. They hatch adders' eggs and weave the spider's web. . . . For our transgressions are multiplied before Thee, and our sins testify against us; for our transgressions are with us, and we know our iniquities [Isaiah 59:2-5, 12].

In verses 16-17 it says, "And He saw that there was no man, and was astonished that there was no one to intercede; then His own arm brought salvation to Him; and His righteousness upheld Him. And He put on righteousness like a breastplate, and a helmet of salvation on His head; and He put on garments of vengeance for clothing, and wrapped Himself with zeal as a mantle."

This is a picture of Christ. He saw a people lost in sin, and just like the Jews of Jesus' time, they were crying out, "Is there no man? Is there no intercessor?" Christ comes and puts on the garments of salvation and, in verse 20, "a Redeemer will come to Zion."

If they had known Isaiah 59, they would have known the answer to their own question. If they had really believed Ezekiel 36, they would have known the Messiah was going to come and wash the inside of His people. First Samuel 16:7 reminded them that "Man looks at the outward appearance, but the LORD looks at the heart."

We can never be in God's kingdom, never enter God's presence, never have His forgiveness, never know the Redeemer, never know salvation, and die frustrated in our sins, unless our hearts are pure. The wonder of it is that this is exactly what Jesus Christ has come to do, to purify our hearts.

When He died on the cross, He took the sin that was accounted to us and paid all the penalty. The Bible says He then imputed His righteousness to us. It's a fantastic exchange. He takes our sin and gives us His righteousness. When we put our faith in Jesus Christ, and God looks at us, He sees us pure. Under no other condition does He see us that way.

Ephesians 1:5 puts it this way, "To the praise of the glory of His grace, which He freely bestowed on us in the Beloved." It is because Christ took our place, bore our sins in His own body on the tree, that His righteousness is given to us. By faith, God makes us pure.

That was His message, and that was the context of it.

What does it mean to be pure in heart?

In the Bible, the heart is always seen as the inside part of man, the seat of his personality. Predominantly, it refers to the thinking process. The heart is not specifically the emotions. When the Bible speaks of the emotions, it often refers to the "bowels of compassion," the "feeling in the stomach," in the midsection. The Jew expressed his feeling in terms of what he felt in his stomach. When he really had some emotion, it turned his stomach.

The mind and the heart were really together. "As he thinketh in his heart, so is he" (Proverbs 23:7, KJV). Sometimes the word *heart* does refer to the will and the emotion as they spin off from the intellect. For example, if my mind is really committed to something, it will affect my will, which will affect my emotion. The will is like a flywheel. The mind sets it going, and once the flywheel moves it generates the emotions.

Proverbs 4:23 pulls this all together: "Watch over your heart with all diligence, for from it flow the springs of life." In other words, whatever the heart is, it is the source of the springs of life. The issues of thinking and feeling and acting all spawn out of this heart. Ephesians 6 talks about doing the will of God from sincerity of heart. It is the point at which everything is generated.

When our Lord is speaking here of the pure in heart, He is thinking first of all of the mind, which controls the will, which controls the responses of emotion. This was a direct shot at the Pharisees and the legalists who were telling everyone that all they needed to take care of was the outside. Jesus was coming right at them.

God is after a changed heart. What did David say in Psalm 51:10? "Create in me a clean heart, O God." "Truly," says Psalm 73:1, "Surely God is good to Israel." Ah, but who in Israel? "To those who are pure in heart!"

If you go to church every day of the week, carry a Bible around and recite verses, but your heart is not clean, you have not met God's standard. Let me illustrate this truth by David and Saul.

When God called Saul to be king, Saul was tall, dark, and handsome, but not much else. So it says in 1 Samuel 10:9 that God gave Saul another heart. He had to change him on the inside. But Saul began to disobey God, and it got to the place where Samuel came to him and said, in effect, "Saul, the Lord says you're finished. You will have no kingly line." (See 1 Samuel 15.) Why? "The LORD has sought out for Himself a man after His own heart" (1 Samuel 13:14).

Why does God care about that? The answer comes again in 1 Samuel 16:7, "For man looks at the outward appearance, but the LORD looks at the heart." Who was the man after God's own heart? David. God selected him because his heart was right. David said in Psalm 9:1, "I will give thanks to the LORD with all my heart."

In Psalm 19:14 David said, "Let the words of my mouth and the meditation of my heart be acceptable in Thy sight, O LORD, my rock and my redeemer." In Psalm 26:2 David cried out, "Examine me, O LORD, and try me; test my mind and my heart." In Psalm 27:8 David says, "When Thou didst say, 'Seek My face,' my heart said to Thee, 'Thy face, O LORD I shall seek.' "

Here was a man who was ruled from his heart. Psalm 28:7 says, "The LORD is my strength and my shield; my heart trusts in Him." David in his innermost being sought God. And do you know what the sum of it all is? Psalm 57:7 declares, "My heart is steadfast, O God, my heart is steadfast." That's the kind of worship God wants, a heart that is fixed on Him. David may have failed on the outside often, but not when his heart was set toward God.

The second term in that phrase "pure in heart" is the word *pure, katharos* in the Greek. You don't talk about purity in our world and become very popular. People think that purity is some flat, insipid, pedestrian, rather vague, unattractive commodity that belongs to strange people in long robes who live in monasteries.

Katharos is a noun form from *katharidzo*, which means to cleanse from filth and iniquity. It means to be free from sin. It is akin to the Latin word *castus*, root of the English word *chaste*. Medical people know that a cathartic is an agent used to cleanse a wound or infected area in order to make it pure. When somebody goes to a psychologist or a counselor, and they have a catharsis, they have a soul cleansing. Interestingly, there are two shades of meaning. Some suggest that it also means unmixed or unalloyed or unadulterated or sifted or cleansed of chaff. In other words, to be pure means you have no added mixture of any foreign element. Thus, what our Lord is really saying here is, "I desire a heart that is unmixed in its devotion and motivation. Pure motives from a pure heart."

Either way, it has to do with attitudes, integrity, and singleness of heart as opposed to duplicity and double-mindedness. Jeremiah 32:39 says, "And I will give them one heart and one way, that they may fear Me always." Psalm 78:72 says of David, "He shepherded them according to the integrity of his heart." That's single devotion, single purpose, pure motive.

Our Lord really emphasizes that principle, as we see later in the Sermon on the Mount, in chapter six: "Where your treasure is, there will your heart be also" (v. 21). He sums it up in verse 24: "No one can serve two masters." James talks about it in his epistle: "Cleanse your hands, you sinners; and purify your hearts, you double-minded" (James 4:8).

Paul is saying in Romans 7, "I have pure motives, even when I can't override my sinful flesh." If you are truly a Christian, that motive for purity should be in your life. If one does not have it in his heart, I question whether he knows God. Do you have that desire in your heart? Do you have pure motives?

The great John Bunyan, who wrote the classics *The Pilgrim's Progress* and *The Holy War,* was once said to have been told by someone how great a preacher he was and that he had no doubt preached a masterpiece that day. Supposedly he sadly replied, "Thank you, but the devil already told me that as I was coming down the pulpit steps."

Pure motive does not stop short of pure deeds. The word *katharos* goes beyond motive. A lot of people with pure motives never come to God. In Mexico City I watched people at the Shrine of Guadalupe crawl on their knees for three hundred yards until they were bleeding. Very sincere, but wrong.

No doubt the worshipers of Baal in Elijah's day had some sincerity when they got out there with knives and started hacking themselves up. I'd say that's sincerity. You start cutting yourself up and you mean business. But there's more than that in the word *katharos.* It is not just a pure motive; it is a holy deed (as defined by God). They both have to be there.

Purity of deed issues out of a pure motive. Thomas Watson said, "Morality can drown a man as fast as vice." He said, "A vessel may sink with gold or with dung." (Watson, *The Beatitudes,* p. 175.) You can say, "I'm a very religious person and want to please God," but if your deeds are not according to His Word, and they do not reveal a real purity, it does not matter.

There are five kinds of purity.

• *Primitive purity.* This is the kind of purity that exists only in God. It is as essential in God as light is to the sun, as wet is to water.

• *Created purity.* This is the creation of a pure being, before the Fall. God created angels in purity, and He created man in purity. They both fell.

• *Ultimate purity.* This is the category of glorification. Ultimately all the saints of God will be completely pure. We are going to have all our sins washed away, not just positionally but practically. First John 3:2 tells us, "We shall be like Him, because we shall see Him just as He is."

- *Positional purity*. This is the purity we have now by the imputation of the righteousness of Christ. When you believe in Jesus Christ, God imputes to you positional purity. When God looks at a Christian He says, believe it or not, "You are right, absolutely pure, in Christ." Romans 3 says the righteousness of Christ has been imputed to us. Romans 5 says we have been justified because of what Christ has done. Galatians 2:16 and 2 Corinthians 5:21 say the same thing.

- *Practical purity*. This is the hard part. Only God knows primitive purity. Only God can bestow created purity. Some day God will give every saint ultimate purity. Right now, every saint has positional purity. But we have a lot of trouble trying to live out what we are in position, don't we? That's why the apostle Paul cried out in 2 Corinthians 7:1, "Let us cleanse ourselves from all defilement of flesh and spirit, perfecting holiness in the fear of God."

He's talking about practical purity, living purity. At best it will be a white cloak with some black thread, but God wants us to be as practically pure as we can be before Him. It is those people who are positionally pure in Jesus Christ who will see God, and those kinds of people will manifest purity of life and purity of motive. If that is not true either the person is not a Christian, or he is living in disobedience.

Certainly we fail, but the Bible tells us how to deal with failure. If we're going to be tempted to be impure, we're going to be tempted to have impure thoughts, say impure words, do impure things, and have impure motives. That will issue in words and deeds that are not right. But the Bible tells us how to deal with temptation. Read Ephesians 6 and get your armor on. That is preventative.

You say, "But what if I fail? First John 1:9 says, "If we confess our sins, He is faithful and righteous to forgive us our sins and to cleanse us from all unrighteousness." Every time you face sin and repent, God cleanses us. It's tremendous to know that God makes us pure.

How can your heart be made pure?

Know you can't do it on your own, that's the first step. There's no way. Proverbs 20:9 asks, "Who can say, 'I have cleansed my heart, I am pure from my sin'?" Nobody.

Acts 15:9 says that our hearts are cleansed by faith. You cannot do it by works, but you can by believing. In what? See 1 John 1:7, in which we are told, "If we walk in the light as He Himself is in the light, we have fellowship with one another, and the blood of Jesus Christ His Son cleanses us from all sin." Faith in what? In the blood of Jesus Christ, which cleanses us from sin.

Do you want to be pure in heart? Then accept the sacrifice of Christ on the cross. Accept what he has already done. Zechariah 13:1 says, "A fountain will be opened . . . for sin and for impurity."

If you are already a Christian, purify your heart through the words of Jesus and through prayer. John 15:3 says, "You are already clean because of the word." Stay in the Word and pray. Hear the words of Job who said, "Who can make the clean out of the unclean?" (Job 14:4). Only one answer echoes down through eternity: "God can."

What is the promise attached to such purity?

What happens if you're pure? The end of the Beatitude: ". . . they shall see God." This is a future form in Greek, a future continuous tense. In other words: "They shall be continually seeing God for themselves." Do you know what happens when your heart is purified at salvation? You live in the presence of God.

You comprehend Him, you realize that He is there, you

see Him with the spiritual eye. Like Moses who cried, "I pray Thee, show me Thy glory" (Exodus 33:18), the one whose heart is purified by Jesus Christ sees again and again the glory of God. To see God was the greatest thing a person in the Old Testament could dream of. Purity of heart cleanses the eyes of the soul so that God is visible.

Do you want to see God? Do you want to have God alive in your world, now and forever? Purify your heart. Some day you will see God with your physical eyes (1 John 3:2). Oh, what a day that will be, to see Christ face to face!

"Happy Are   9
the Peacemakers. . ."

Matthew 5:9

"Blessed are the peacemakers, for they shall be called sons of God."

The idea of peace dominates the Bible. It opens with peace in the Garden of Eden and closes with peace in eternity. In fact, you could chart the course of biblical history by the peace theme. Man's sin interrupted peace in the Garden. At the cross, Christ became our peace. (Because He has provided peace, there can be peace in the heart of a man or woman who comes to know Him.) Some day He will come again, and His title will be fulfilled as the "Prince of Peace." He will establish an eternal kingdom of peace.

In the Bible there are four hundred references to peace. God calls Himself the "God of Peace," but there is no peace in the world. True. And there are two reasons: the opposition of Satan, and the disobedience of men. The fall of some of the angels and the fall of man has caused a world without peace.

It isn't that God does not want peace. God is not at war with man. God is not even at war with the fallen angels. But the fallen angels and man are at war with God. As long as they will have no peace, there will be none.

Now we come to the seventh step in the ladder that ascends to divine blessedness, which we have translated *happiness*. It almost seems that God has called us to restore and to experience something lost since the Fall. We are to restore this world to the peace that was forfeited by our sinning. A special people whom he calls peacemakers are His agents in the world, and they are here to go far beyond anyone who wins the Nobel Peace Prize, because the peace they offer is eternal, divine, real.

Jesus says God has promised to bless people who are His agents for peace, and even to call them "sons of God."

The world's peacemakers have a terrible record. The peace we hail today begins to collapse tomorrow. We do not have political peace, economic peace, social peace, or domestic peace. We have peace nowhere because we have no peace in our hearts. That's the real issue. Someone has said, "Washington has lots of peace monuments. They build one after each war."

Peace is merely that brief glorious moment in history when everybody stops to reload. The world was concerned in the aftermath of World War II with developing an agency for world peace, so in 1945 the United Nations brought itself into existence with the motto: "To have succeeding generations free from the scourge of war." Since that time there has not been one day of peace on the earth. Not one. It's a pipe dream.

There is no peace. We have no ability to get along with each other. Every relationship is fragile. People have mental and emotional illnesses as never before. There are family breakups, disorders in schools. There seems no end to it. Man has no peace in himself, so his world, which is merely a projection of himself, is riddled with chaos.

In the wonderful verse we are studying in this chapter, God says He will especially bless those who are peacemakers. To understand what our Lord is saying here, we must deal with five truths about peace, five realities.

The meaning of peace

Some people define peace as the absence of conflict or strife. No conflict or strife exists in a cemetery, but we don't look there for a model of God's peace. As God sees it, peace is far more than the absence of something. It is the presence of righteousness that causes right relationships. Peace is not just stopping war; peace is creating righteousness that brings enemies together in love.

When a Jew says to another Jew, "Shalom," he doesn't mean, "May you have no war." He means, "May you have all the righteousness and goodness God can give."

There's a big difference between a truce and peace. A truce just says you don't shoot for a while. Peace comes when the truth is known, the issue is settled, and the parties embrace each other. Stopping a war just makes it boil. Approaching peace that way may develop a far worse situation.

The peace of the Bible never evades issues. The peace of the Bible is not peace at any price. It is not a gloss. The peace of the Bible conquers the problem. It builds a bridge. Sometimes it means struggle, sometimes it means pain, sometimes it means anguish, but in the end, real peace can come. Biblical peace is real peace.

James 3:17 says, "But the wisdom from above is first pure, then peaceable." Peace is never sought at the expense of righteousness. You have not made peace between two people unless they have seen the sin, the error, and the wrongness of the bitterness and hatred and have resolved to bring it before God and make it right. Then peace comes through purity.

Hebrews 12:14 says, "Pursue peace with all men, and the sanctification without which no one will see the Lord." You cannot divorce peace from purity. You cannot divorce peace from righteousness (Psalm 85:10). We all want to avoid needless strife, whether at home, at work, or wherever, but if we avoid it to the point of sacrificing truth, then we compromise our principles, and we don't have peace at all—we have just a truce, a ceasefire, a cold war, a time to reload.

Our Lord said in Matthew 10:34, "Do not think that I came to bring peace on the earth; I did not come to bring peace, but a sword," which seems diametrically opposed to this Beatitude. What He means is that He did not come to bring peace at any price. He knew there had to be strife before there could be peace.

Often I have said this about preaching the gospel. You have to get them mad at you before you can get them happy with you. You have to upset them before you can make them better. You have to make them feel bad before you can ever make them feel good. So it is in bringing a true peace to the world. First a sword falls and out of the sword can come peace, because it is the sword of purity, the sword of righteousness, the sword of holiness. Jude, verse 3 supports this when it says, "Beloved, while I was making every effort to write you about our common salvation, I felt the necessity to write to you appealing that you contend earnestly for the faith which was once for all delivered to the saints."

We have to be contentious about some things. So, we bring the gospel to bear, and it ruffles feathers, it convicts, it brings contention and strife. But when the conflict is resolved by faith in Jesus Christ, there is real peace. We are not to abandon doctrine or conviction, and we are not to avoid bringing up truth just because it offends somebody.

On the contrary, we must bring it up, and let it offend so the person can get to real peace. If you deal with truth, you'll be a divider, a disturber, a disrupter. There is no way around it.

We have all tried to live for Christ and give our testimony. All of a sudden there you are trying to be a peacemaker, helping people make peace with God and each other and in their own hearts, and all they do is get angry at you. The whole premise of your message is that they have to deal with sin, and people do not like to hear that. Thus they put up a barrier to peace.

While we could call a truce during such a situation, we would not be helping the individual make peace with God. Biblical peacemakers are not quiet, easy-going people who just want to make no waves or no issues, who lack justice and a sense of righteousness, who are compromisers and appeasers. People say, "Oh, he's such a peacemaker," when they really mean, "He has no conviction."

A true biblical peacemaker will not let sleeping dogs lie, he will not save the status quo. He does not say, "I know the person's doing wrong, but I would rather just have a peaceful situation. I just want to keep the peace." That's a cop-out.

So, the meaning of peace is resolving conflict by the truth, as you bring to bear the righteousness of God.

The menace to peace

What is it that hinders peace? If the meaning of peace is righteousness and truth, then the menace to peace is error and lies. Jeremiah 17:9 says, "The heart is more deceitful than all else and is desperately sick." Now get that. How does a wicked heart manifest itself? Isaiah 48:22, "There is no peace for the wicked, says the LORD." Jeremiah says man's heart is deceitful, and Isaiah says he shall have no peace because of it.

What we must face, then, is an internally defiled man, a man from whom proceeds evil. That kind of heart can never produce peace, because peace is a result of holiness and righteousness. That's why James 3:18 says, "The seed whose fruit is righteousness is sown in peace by those who make peace." Peacemakers sow righteous fruit.

If two people are fighting, it's because of sin. Eliminate the sin and the fight's over. The only real peacemakers in the world are those who bring men to righteousness, to God's standards. All the diplomats, statesmen, ambassadors, presidents, and kings of the world could never bring peace. We cannot be peacemakers unless we follow the first six Beatitudes.

We start with a beggarly attitude toward our own sinfulness (v. 3). We cower in the corner and crouch in the dark, reaching out to God because we know we cannot earn anything on our own. Then we weep and mourn (v. 4), and our heart burns and aches over our sinfulness. We see ourselves before a sovereign and holy God and the meekness (v. 5) is born out of the mourning. We cry out in a hunger and thirst after righteousness (v. 6), and we receive (v. 7) the mercy of God.

Verse 8 says we become pure in heart, and only then can we be a peacemaker (v. 9). When we become peacemakers, the world is not going to accept that, so verse 10 says, "Blessed are those who have been persecuted for the sake of righteousness." Why? Because people do not immediately want to hear about the kind of peace God has to offer. There is too much truth in it.

If you have righteousness, purity, and holiness in your life, you will have peace. And if you have righteousness, purity, and holiness in your marriage, nation, or home, peace will be there, too. Because that's always the way. Once you have righteousness, you are at peace with God, with man, and with yourself.

How marvelous it is to see how God uses the simplest and humblest people to be the peacemakers of the world. He exalts people who never win the prizes or get their names in the headlines. We must be the ones bringing righteousness to bear in an individual so that his heart knows peace for the first time. We must be the ones bringing righteousness to bear on a relationship so that a couple can know peace. We must be the ones preaching the gospel so that men can know peace with God.

Jesus was the greatest peacemaker of all, but did He avoid conflict? Hardly. They killed Him. But He did it because He knew that peace would be found in the end. Man can search the world over, go from counselor to counselor, gather at summit after summit, write treaty after treaty, and go from religion to religion, and never find peace. Why? Because peace is not to be found in our human reason or in our circumstances.

In our world, we often exalt the people who break peace, not the ones who make it. Have you noticed that? We will pay a fortune to watch two men in a ring beat each other to a pulp. Worldly kingdoms have always given the highest honor to the warriors. We bow to the great god of macho. The virile, the "take-nothin'-from-nobody," the hard-nosed, the tough, the wild, the self-sufficient. Those are the heroes.

The heroines are the women who lead the fight for rights and make demands, who stir up strife and contention and fight traditions.

We are a whole society of people fighting for our rights and exalting ourselves. We are told by psychologists and psychiatrists and behaviorists, "Get all you can for yourself. Don't let anybody take anything from you." It's no wonder that when Christians try to bring the peace of the gospel to this society, they are fought.

No wonder the Jews did not like Jesus Christ. They wanted a fighter. When He said, "Blessed are the peacemakers," I'm sure the people of that day really rolled their eyes. So today people may look down on Christians and think them cowardly and weak. If they get bold and really preach Christ, people fight them.

We can't feel bad about having some enemies, as long as they're the right enemies. Jesus Christ was the Prince of Peace and yet He created conflict. (See Luke 23:5.) Paul the apostle, who said that he was preaching the message of man's reconciliation to God, the "gospel of peace" he called it, created a riot nearly every place he went!

We have to be willing to enter the conflict, to take the blows like Christ did, to take up our cross, to deny ourselves, to pay the price, to be bold and charge right through with what we know is right. If we bow out of the tough situations, we cannot be peacemakers.

When I see a person living in sin, and if I were really a peacemaker, as Jesus would want me to be, I must go to that person and say, "You're offending a holy God. You are, by your very life, at war with God. I want to make peace between you and God, and so I'm confronting you with your sin and offering you the gospel of Jesus Christ."

Now, that's bold. If I see two Christians fighting, it is not right to skirt the issue. A real peacemaker says, "You must resolve this righteously with one another." Being a peacemaker is not avoiding the issue, it's diving right into the middle of it and trying to bring about a righteous solution.

The maker of peace

Who is the maker of peace? Paul said it directly in 1 Corinthians 14:33: "For God is not a God of confusion but of peace." God is the author, the maker, the source of peace. Apart from Him, there is no peace. The New Testament is replete with statements that God is the God of peace. Paul said in Romans 15:33, "Now the God of peace be with you all." In 2 Thessalonians 3:16 he talks about Christ as the "Lord of peace." The author of Hebrews writes about the "God of peace" (13:20).

Since the Fall in Genesis 3, man has never known peace unless he has taken it as a gift from God. God is at perfect peace with Himself. The Trinity has perfect oneness. Ephesians 2:14 says, "For He Himself [Christ] is our peace."

I remember reading the story of a couple arguing back and forth in a divorce hearing. Their four-year-old boy was teary-eyed watching the conflict. According to the article, he took his father's hand, then his mother's hand, and kept pulling until he pulled the two hands together. He became a peacemaker.

In a sense, that's what Christ did for us. He provided the

righteousness that allows man to take the hand of God. Colossians 1:20 says that Jesus Christ was able "to reconcile all things to Himself, having made peace through the blood of His cross. The cross made peace, though there was no peace at the cross. It was a chaotic scene, but the cross provided the righteousness that alone makes real peace.

So, God is the source of peace; Jesus is the manifestation of peace; and the Holy Spirit is the agency of peace. Galatians 5:22 says, "The fruit of the Spirit is love, joy, peace."

God does not want conflict. People say, "What kind of a God do we have? Look at all the wars!" God does not want those wars. Why doesn't He stop them? He didn't start them. They are not His wars. In Jeremiah 29:11 the prophet said, "For I know the plans that I have for you, declares the LORD, plans for welfare and not for calamity."

Jesus said, "These things I have spoken to you, that in Me you may have peace. In the world you have tribulation, but take courage; I have overcome the world." We Christians can abide in the Lord, and peace is there. No matter how much anxiety and turmoil there is in the world, there is a cushion of peace, an eye in the storm, in the soul of the person who knows the Prince of Peace, the one who has the indwelling Spirit of peace, given by the God of peace.

The messengers of peace

We are the messengers of peace. First Corinthians 7:15 says, "God has called us to peace." Second Corinthians 5:18-20 tells us, "Now all these things are from God, who reconciled us to Himself through Christ, and gave us the ministry of reconciliation [peacemaking], namely, that God was in Christ reconciling the world to Himself, not counting their trespasses against them, and He has committed to us the word of reconciliation. Therefore, we are ambassadors for Christ, as though God were entreating through us; we beg you on behalf of Christ, be reconciled to God."

We are God's peace corps in the truest sense. Many other

Scriptures talk about this: Colossians 3:15, "Let the peace of Christ rule in your hearts"; Philippians 4:7, "The peace of God . . . shall guard your hearts and your minds in Christ Jesus."

You might ask, "As a peacemaker, what do I do?" Three things:

1. Make peace with God yourself. Accept the gospel of peace. As Paul put it in Ephesians 6:15, "Having shod your feet with the preparation of the gospel of peace." There was a day when we warred against God, but when Jesus Christ's righteousness was imputed to us, we made peace with God. The battle's over.

We have to maintain that peace. Every time there is sin in our lives, that peace is interrupted, and we cannot commune freely with God. We are to get sin confessed quickly so there will be peace between us and God again.

2. Help others make peace with God. The greatest thing about peacemaking is that we can go to somebody who's at war with God and make peace between that person and God. The minute he comes to Jesus Christ and makes peace with God, he'll be at peace with us. He becomes God's child and our brother.

Evangelism is peacemaking. The best way to be a peacemaker is to preach the gospel of peace so that a man's alienation from God and from the body of Christ can be ended and he can be at peace. No wonder it says in Romans 10:15, "How beautiful are the feet of those who bring glad tidings of good things!" Do you really want to be a peacemaker? Tell somebody about Jesus Christ.

The self-righteous, smug Pharisees thought they had every right to fight Rome, to spout their theology, and to step on people's necks. They created strife everywhere they went. They looked down on people and divided society into cliques and groups. Jesus says to such people, "You've got it all wrong. What God wants is not some spiritual elite but some poor, beggarly sinner who knows he has got nothing to offer and who seeks to make peace."

3. Make peace with men; bring them together with each other. It's not always easy, but a peacemaker can build bridges between people. Jesus says, "If therefore you are presenting your offering at the altar, and there remember that your brother has something against you [Not that you have something against your brother, but that he has something against you!], leave your offering there before the altar, and go your way; first be reconciled to your brother, and then come and present your offering" (Matthew 5:23-24).

God does not want folks coming to church and worshipping Him if they know somebody has something against them. Later in Matthew 5 Jesus talks about how we are to love even our enemies, bless them that curse us, do good to them that hate us, and pray for them that despitefully use us and persecute us. Why? Because then we shall prove to be "sons of your Father" (Matthew 5:48).

We will show that we're sons of God if we're peacemakers, even with our enemies. The Beatitude says peacemakers are happy, "for they shall be called sons of God." Sometimes there's a tremendous price to pay, and sometimes it's even impossible. That's why the apostle Paul says in Romans 12:18, "If *possible*, so far as it depends on you, be at peace with all men."

Sometimes people don't cooperate, but that doesn't change the fact that we have to make the effort. Jesus said in Mark 9:50, "Be at peace with one another." That means between you and your spouse, too, doesn't it? If you're having trouble with your worship, maybe you need to get straightened out with your wife or husband at home. Otherwise, according to 1 Peter 3:7, your prayers are going to be hindered. There must be real peace, not just, "All right, Ethel, we won't talk about that anymore, especially on the way to church—we're supposed to be worshipping this morning!" That's not peace; that's a cold war. You need to resolve such a problem.

Be a peacemaker. Maybe it will cost you, and maybe you will have to suffer some, but that's what a peacemaker does. That's what Jesus did, and He is our example.

We should consciously work on being peacemakers. I try even in situations in which someone and I do not have any bitterness between us (there's nothing but love) but we disagree in theology. Every time we're together I don't say, "I've got some more stuff I'm going to tell you!" I don't carry a load of tapes of my viewpoint on something and say, "The Lord told me to tell you to listen to this, brother." No. I always try to find the point of agreement, the point of peace, because once you have established peace, you can build on it.

The merit of peace

You might also question the results of being a peacemaker. What happens? According to the Beatitude, you shall be called a son of God. I couldn't think of a better thing to be called, could you?

I'm glad I'm a MacArthur. That's a great, old Scottish family. There was a good general with that name and even a millionaire (Which hasn't helped me one bit!). I'm happy to be my father's son, and I'm happy to be the grandson of a great man of God. But nothing, I mean nothing, compares to being a son of God.

The merit that belongs to the peacemakers is that of God's sons. The Greek uses *huios* for *sons*, not *tekna*, which means *children*. *Tekna* speaks of tender affection. *Huios* speaks of dignity and honor and standing. So Christ is not talking merely about the affection that belongs to us; He's talking about the dignity and the honor of being a son of God!

As a father, I love my children more than I love my house. God's house is the universe, and He loves me more than He loves that. I love my children more than my estate. Jacob prized Benjamin more than everything he owned. Genesis 44:30 tells us that Jacob's life was all bound up in Benjamin.

So it is with God as His great love is all bound up with you and me.

We're His sons. The Bible says we're the apple of His eye. We immediately think of some shiny little apple. But what the Hebrew meant by the apple of the eye was the pupil, the most vulnerable part of the body. It's the tenderest part, the most sensitive part. You protect it. When anything comes toward your eye's pupil, you shield it.

God feels that way about His children. You touch one of His children, and you've poked your finger in His eye. He says in Malachi 3:17 that we are His jewels. Isaiah 56:5 says that He will give us an everlasting name. Psalm 56:8 says He keeps our tears in His bottle. Isn't that fabulous? An old Hebrew custom when you cried over something was to store your tears in a bottle so people would know how you sorrowed. God keeps our tears in His bottle so that He'll know the sorrow we've been through.

When we die, this truth becomes the most wonderful thing of all. Psalm 116:15 says, "Precious in the sight of the LORD is the death of His godly ones." We really matter to God. We are His sons. He makes us princes, kings, priests, fellow heirs. In Psalm 16:3 He calls us the "majestic ones." In 2 Timothy 2:21 a "vessel for honor." Revelation says we shall get to sit with Him on His throne! Like children jumping up on the lap of a father.

Have you ever considered what it means to be a son of God? God has a personal, eternal love for you. God bears with your weakness and your sin. God accepts your imperfect service. God provides for your every need, shields you from every danger, reveals to you His eternal truth. He forgives you and keeps on forgiving you every sin.

God makes you an heir to everything He possesses. God works everything for your good. He keeps you from perishing forever. And He gives you heaven.

You can tell such a son of God—he's a peacemaker.

10
"Happy Are the Harassed. . ."
—Part one
Matthew 5:10-12

"Blessed are those who have been persecuted for the sake of righteousness, for theirs is the kingdom of heaven. Blessed are you when men revile you, and persecute you, and say all kinds of evil against you falsely, on account of Me. Rejoice, and be glad, for your reward in heaven is great, for so they persecuted the prophets who were before you."

It fascinates me that the believer who lives in the Beatitudes will be both a peacemaker and one who creates persecution. You hear it from the lips of the Lord Jesus Christ regarding Himself, when He said that He came as the Prince of Peace, yet "not come to bring peace, but a sword" (Matthew 10:34).

After studying the Beatitudes and realizing that they are the characteristics of the man or the woman in God's kingdom, it is easy to feel inadequate, isn't it? This kind of person seems a little too good to be true, like somebody on a stained glass window, or a plaster saint. Surely nobody lives this way in everyday life; nobody could fulfill all those incredible characteristics!

Then is God dealing with wood and stone and glass saints here? I think not. I believe that what Jesus presents here in this introduction to the Sermon on the Mount is no less than the portrait of a believer, no less than the picture of the genuine Christian. Of course it's ideal. God never lowers His standards just because man is sinful. God simply gives Christ to the individual so that Christ can work through him in meeting God's standard.

As we have seen, the person who lives these principles is truly happy, really blessed, one who knows bliss. Every one of us who is genuinely born again must have come to Jesus Christ with these attitudes, however simple and under-developed the attitudes might have been. They must have been manifest in our lives to some extent. Therefore, we should see more of them every day we live, until we finally pass into the fullness and the richness of kingdom character.

Maybe we fulfill these characteristics in only a minimal way, but originally we had to come with a broken spirit, mourning over sin, humble before a holy God, hungering and thirsting for righteousness, seeking mercy and a pure heart, desiring to make peace with God. If these things existed, however minimally, you entered into His kingdom.

Now these should bloom and progress until they become more than minimal, but rather the dominant characteristics in your life.

When this happens, that the eighth Beatitude will always be true: "Blessed are those who have been persecuted for the sake of righteousness, for theirs is the kingdom of heaven." When we begin to live the way God wants us to live, we find pain and suffering. We will be peacemakers, yes, but we will be troublemakers, too.

James 1:2-4 says, "Consider it all joy, my brethren, when you encounter various trials, knowing that the testing of your faith produces endurance. And let endurance have its perfect result, that you may be perfect and complete, lacking in nothing." 1 Peter 5:10 says, "And after you have *suffered* for a little while, the God of all grace, who called you to His eternal glory in Christ, will Himself perfect, confirm, strengthen and establish you."

All the virtues of the Beatitude character are intolerable to an evil world. The world cannot handle somebody who is poor in spirit, because the world lives in pride, in a state of self-promotion and ego-substantiation. The world cannot tolerate mourning over sinfulness. It wants to bypass sin altogether and convince itself that it's all right. The world cannot tolerate meekness; it honors pride. The world cannot tolerate someone who knows he is nothing and seeks something that cannot be earned. The world knows little about mercy, about purity, about making peace. These characteristics flagrantly counter the system.

A few years ago, *Cosmopolitan* magazine (February 1978) conducted a test to determine how happy people really are. As a result of its survey, the magazine drew this profile of truly happy people:

They enjoy other people, but are not self-sacrificing. They refuse to participate in any negative feelings or emotions. They have a sense of accomplishment based on their own self-sufficiency.

Fascinating. It sounds like the definition of a Pharisee to me. It is certainly opposite to Jesus' definition of a happy person. Jesus said the really happy person is not self-sufficient but cowering like a beggar, realizing he has no resources in himself. He is meek rather than proud. He is not at all positive about himself but is rather mourning over his sinfulness and isolation from a holy God. He is not confident in his own ability, but he is aware of his inability and reaches out in meekness. He is merciful and a peacemaker, even if it costs him persecution.

Nothing could give a clearer picture of the difference between the world's philosophy and divine truth than the preceding comparison. When the world runs into Christianity, there is always conflict, conviction, guilt, resentment, per-

secution. If you function according to the first seven principles in the Beatitudes, inevitably you will be persecuted for
righteousness's sake.

Let's look at three distinct features of this last Beatitude—persecution, promise, and posture.

Persecution

Persecution is general in verse 10, "Blessed are those,"
whereas verse 11 says, "Blessed are you," and personalizes
it. In my opinion, though it is repeated in two verses in
slightly different terms, this is all one Beatitude. The term
persecuted is used in verse 10 and again in verse 11, but
expanded. Also, only one result is listed, and that's at the
end of verse 10, "theirs is the kingdom of heaven."

So, if only one Beatitude is in view, why does it have two
blesseds? I believe God doubly blesses those who suffer and
those who are persecuted. And who is involved? Who are
those who are persecuted for righteousness's sake and reviled "for My sake"? The text does not say, but it's easy to
figure.

The blessed ones of verses 10 and 11 are the same blessed
ones of verses 3 through 9. There is no change in character;
it is the people who have lived out the Beatitudes, the kingdom people. To the degree that you fulfill the first seven
Beatitudes, you will experience the eighth.

Second Timothy 3 is a picture of the future, yet it's certainly pertinent to us. In verse 11 it says, "persecutions,
sufferings, such as happened to me [Paul] at Antioch, at
Iconium and at Lystra; what persecutions I endured, and out
of them all the Lord delivered me!" Paul says he was persecuted as one who lived a kingdom life, one who manifested
Jesus Christ.

In verse 12, he adds, "And indeed, all who desire to live
godly in Christ Jesus will be persecuted." This is a gilt-
edged guarantee that anybody who lives out the Christ-like
character will suffer. In Galatians 4:29, Paul says simply,

"But as at that time he who was born according to the flesh persecuted him who was born according to the Spirit, so it is now also." Nothing has changed. We will get along terrifically if nobody ever finds out we are Christians, but as we begin to live the Christ-life, as we begin to manifest the Beatitudes, as we share the reproach of Jesus Christ, as we participate in the fellowship of His sufferings, and as we live righteously in the world, we will find that the sons of the flesh will always persecute the ones born of the Spirit.

Living in direct opposition to Satan in his world and system will inevitably bring antagonism and persecution from the people who do not respond to our message. Christlikeness produces the same reaction it did when He was on earth. There was never anyone more loving or a greater peacemaker than Jesus Christ. Some people responded to that love, and some people even entered into His peace. But even though Jesus was the most loving, magnanimous, gracious, kind, peaceful person who ever lived, everywhere He went He created antagonism.

Why? Because He was confrontive about the issues. Chart the course of the righteous through history, and it becomes very clear that they have always suffered for their godliness. It started when righteous Abel was murdered by an ungodly brother who simply could not tolerate his righteousness. There was always a price.

Thomas Watson, the Puritan writer, perceives this when he writes, "Though they be never so meek, merciful, pure in heart, their piety will never shield them from suffering. They must hang their harp on the willows and take the cross. The way to heaven is by the way of thorns and blood. . . . Set it down as a maxim, if you will follow Christ, you will see the swords and staves. Put the cross in your creed." (Thomas Watson, *The Beatitudes*, p. 259).

Actually, one of the most wonderful guarantees that our salvation is real is to be persecuted. Philippians 1:29 says, "For to you it has been granted for Christ's sake, not only to

believe in Him, but also to suffer for His sake." Now, notice
also that Philippians 1:28 says, "In no way alarmed by your
opponents—which is a sign of destruction for them."

In other words, when our adversaries come against us,
hating the gospel, hating Christ in you, and resenting the
character of kingdom living, it is a sign of their destiny,
proof that they are bound for hell. But to us it is an evident
sign of salvation. Living the redeemed life and seeing the
antagonism of a godless world is evidence that our salvation
is genuine.

In 1 Thessalonians 3:3, the apostle Paul says "that no man
may be disturbed by these afflictions." We should not be
worried or fearful if we are persecuted. Why? "For you
yourselves know that we have been destined for this." This
is the design of God. We are to be like Christ, loved and
hated, honored and cursed. Paul goes on in verse 4, "For
indeed when we were with you, we kept telling you in
advance that we were going to suffer affliction; and so it
came to pass, as you know."

He's saying that this is part of becoming a Christian. It
was ordained. You knew it was given to you to suffer for the
sake of Christ, and when they persecute you it is an evident
sign of their own perdition.

If we don't have any persecution in our lives, we'd better
examine our claim to be Christians. If I'm not cause for flak
in the world, if I'm not making waves, if I'm not generating
some sort of a conflict, then maybe something's seriously
wrong.

We have lived in a rather tolerant time in North America
in terms of public or governmental persecution. That seems
to be changing. But wherever you live a redeemed life to its
hilt, wherever you live out the principles of the kingdom
life, wherever you are an obedient son of the kingdom, living the righteousness of Christ in this world, it will come to
be obnoxious to Satan. Always.

Just because we think the attitude of the world has

changed, Christians may pride themselves because they are popular. In many cases Christians are famous, Christians are accepted, Christians are paraded about and made a part of our society, without any hassles at all. But the issue is not that the world has changed. The issue is that we have lowered the standard of righteousness, and we have people who claim to be Christians who do not live enough of a righteous life to give an honest definition of Christianity—otherwise, the systems they are engulfed in would spit them right out.

We think the world is just more tolerant, but the fact is, we may not be living intolerable lives. We want to be popular, we want to be famous, we want to be acceptable. But, if you live the righteous life God asks you to live, the world can only resent and hate you. I must add that this does not mean that every one of us is going to know constant persecution all our lives. Christ is simply saying that the world will pick out some of us. All of us who live righteously in the world, at some time or another, are going to know the rebuke of the cross. Which is worse, being burned at the stake or living your whole life, say, in a business in which you can never get the promotion you deserve because the people resent your Christianity? Or always being ostracized from the people around you because you live for Jesus Christ? Or having the people in your neighborhood not talk to you anymore because when you talk to them you don't pander to their evil but rather confront them with it?

Oh, we can escape. We can go through our whole lives and never be persecuted. First, approve the world's standards. Fit right in. Accept the world's morals and ethics. Live like the world lives. Laugh at its jokes, enjoy its entertainment, smile when it mocks God. Let it take His name in vain. Don't tell people they're sinners. Don't tell people they're lost without Jesus Christ. Don't tell people they're doomed to death, and whatever you do, don't mention hell!

I promise you, you shall never be persecuted. And if that is your choice, examine yourself to see whether or not you

are in the faith. You may be a Christian living in disobedience, or you might not be a Christian at all. Just remember
Luke 9:26, where Jesus says, "Whoever is ashamed of Me
and My words, of him will the Son of Man be ashamed." It
can happen. In Luke 6:26 our Lord says this, "Woe to you
when all men speak well of you." Don't ever forget that.
When you are popular with everybody, that means they
don't know the truth about you. Either you have masked
your Christianity, or you are not a Christian at all.

When Jesus gave these Beatitudes early in His ministry,
He was already hated. In Mark 3:6 the Pharisees went forth
and "immediately began taking counsel with the Herodians
against Him, as to how they might destroy Him." He had
hardly articulated the principles of His kingdom, and the
hatred was already beginning to rise. Jesus was saying to
the Pharisees and the lay people in that crowd, "Look, I'm
telling you, up front, right at the beginning, there's a price
to pay to live in My kingdom. It isn't all going to be thrones
and glory and crowns and fame and prestige and acceptance
and everybody loving you and exalting you and lifting you
up. If you're coming into My kingdom, you will suffer. Let it
be known to you."

We need more preaching like that. We need to tell people
that God is calling them to a life contrary to the system of the
world, and that there will be a price to pay. It's going to
affect what they do. It's going to affect how they make their
living. More than one hundred years after the Sermon on the
Mount, a man came to Tertullian and said, "I've come to
Christ, but I don't know what to do. I have a job that I don't
think is right, but I have to live."

To which Tertullian replied, "Must you?" (Quoted in
William Barclay, *The Gospel of Matthew*, 1:106-7.)

The only choice is loyalty to Jesus Christ, even if you must
die. Imagine what loyalty to Christ did to the social lives of
early Christians. Feasts were held in the temples of different
gods. Those were the great social events. That was where

the music was, along with the dancing, the entertainment, the sacrifices. It got so ridiculous that people who brought sacrifices to the gods did not want to waste any meat. They would just wave the sacrifice over the fire and singe the hair on the outer part of it. Then they would whack off some for the priest and keep the rest for a wild party with their friends. When they became Christians they wondered, *What do I do with my friends? Do I go and eat the meat offered to the idols? Do I go to the pagan temple for the entertainment? Or do I pay the price of separation?* We are still making similar choices.

A Jew could be thrown out of the synagogue, even kicked out of his family, deprived of everything he knew.

If we're going to live a kingdom life, we ought to be prepared to be very lonely in some crowds. That's why we need each other so much.

In those early days, too, Christians had to pay a penalty. Some were flung to the lions. Others were burned at the stake. Nero used to light his garden parties with flaming Christians whom he had covered with pitch and had set fire to. He sewed some Christians in the skins of wild animals and sent his hunting dogs to tear them to pieces.

They were tortured on the rack; they were scraped; hissing molten lead was poured on them. Red-hot brass plates were affixed to the tenderest parts of their bodies. Eyes were torn out. Parts of their bodies were cut off and roasted before their eyes. Their hands and feet were burned while cold water was poured over them to lengthen the agony.

The Romans even trumped up charges that the Christians were cannibals, from the words of Jesus to "eat my flesh and drink my blood." They accused the Christians of actually eating each other in their communion observances. They said their love feasts were orgies of lust. They even charged that the kiss of peace was something illicit.

They slandered them for setting fires, blamed them for the burning of Rome, and branded them revolutionaries. Because the Christians were always talking about God's finally destroying the earth in fire, which repeated the message of 2 Peter 3:10, it was easy to blame them when a fire broke out.

There is much to learn about persecution from the early Christians. In the time of Christ the Roman Empire extended all the way from the British Isles to the Euphrates River. All the way from the northern tip of Germany to North Africa. It was massive—the whole known world. The Romans were tremendously concerned about how to unify the empire. They realized that there was one man who was the personification of the whole Roman empire, and that was Caesar, the emperor.

So they decided to make Caesar into a god. If they could get everybody to worship him, ascribing to him divine honor, they would build temples all over the empire to his divinity, and then they would have their cohesive unit. It started very slowly, but after a few years there developed a real emperor-worshipping cult. It was compulsory once each year for every person in the Roman Empire to burn incense to Caesar and say, "Caesar is lord."

When a man burned his incense he was given a certificate called a *libellus*. Once he had that, he could worship any god he wanted. The Romans just wanted to be sure that everyone plugged in at one common point first: Caesar. The Christians would not say anything but "Jesus is Lord," so they never got their *libellus*. Consequently, they were constantly worshipping illegally. (William Barclay, *The Gospel of Matthew*, 1:107-10.)

They chose Christ. They refused to compromise. They became dissidents, rebels, pockets of disloyalty, threats to the empire's solidarity, and one poet spoke of them as "the panting huddling flock whose only crime was Christ." They faced torture for their stand. Do you?

Maybe the reason our Christianity is so tolerable in our society is because our standard is so low. We compromise all the time. Jesus adds to the list of Beatitudes the inevitability of persecution. How are we to be persecuted? Verse 11, "Blessed are you when men revile you, and persecute you, and say all kinds of evil against you falsely, on account of me." There you have the three ways: reviled, persecuted, and all kinds of evil said against you falsely.

Persecuted comes from *dioko* in the Greek, an interesting word that means to pursue, drive, or chase away. It finally came to mean to harass or treat evily. He's simply saying, "Blessed [Happy] are the harassed. Blessed are those who have been persecuted for the sake of righteousness."

This is an attitude, just as all the previous Beatitudes have been attitudes. This is the attitude of being willing to be persecuted. It is that lack of fear, that lack of shame, that presence of boldness that says, "I will be in this world what Christ would have me be. I will say in this world what Christ will have me say. And if persecution results, let it be."

It is a passive participle in the Greek, indicating the permissiveness of those who allow themselves to be persecuted. Blessed are they who allow themselves. . . Since it is a passive perfect participle, the perfect tense means it happened with continuing results. As a result of living a Beatitude kind of life, the believer is constantly willing to accept whatever comes. I guess this is where some of us bail out, isn't it?

I struggle with this myself. I'm not always willing to take what I'm going to get if I say what I ought to say. I'm not always willing to be bold and just confront the situation and say what needs to be said. I'm not always willing to live the Christ-life in the midst of a Christless situation, and so be light and salt in the world. I tend to want to accommodate myself and have the world like me.

Inevitably, I am tempted to justify myself by saying, "If I'm popular with them, and they like me a lot, I can sneak the gospel in." God never needed sneaky preachers, and He doesn't need sneaky prophets. He doesn't need sneaky witnesses and evangelists. He needs those who are willing to confront.

First-century Christians were going to be chased and pursued and harassed, and the result for some was imprisonment and death. If we really live Christ-like lives in this society, we cannot go to the parties with the boys. We cannot do what all the gals in the neighborhood do. We cannot go with some of the couples we used to go with. Neither can we do the things they do. There is something about living the life that Christ wants us to live that causes them to chase us out of the group. We just don't fit anymore. And that's the way it ought to be.

Revile, *oneididzo* in the Greek, means to cast in one's teeth. It was used in the crucifixion of Christ in Matthew 27:44 when they mocked Him, made fun of Him, reviled Him, scorned Him. It's to throw something into one's face, to abuse one with vile, vicious, mocking words.

So, we are not only going to be chased out of the groups we used to be in, but we will also be subject to evil spoken of us. People will say things about us, use unkind words when our names come up. They did it to Jesus (Luke 22:63-65). Some who do this may be people whom we care for very much.

I have always found that I could take a little of the chasing away. Nobody wants me around much after they find that I'm a minister. It's amazing how fast people want to get out of my presence after they find out that I'm not a minister like other ministers they have known—that I'm a little more confrontive.

I have usually been able to handle people's saying unkind and vile things about me. I know what it is to be arrested for preaching. I once preached to some black believers in a certain place in the South. I didn't get very far away from the preaching location before a police car caught up with me, and I was taken to jail. They threatened to strip my clothes off and beat me with a whip if I continued to do what I was doing. That was in the United States of America!

I guess those things I can tolerate. But then there's that third thing, which Christ says people will "say all kinds of evil against you *falsely.*" I don't mind if they don't like me or what I say, but when they claim I say things that I don't say, that's hard to take. Then you try to defend yourself over something you never even said.

They tried to say Jesus was the illegitimate son of a Roman soldier. They have tried to say things about God's people throughout all of history. Arthur W. Pink well says that it's a strong proof of human depravity that men's curses and Christ's blessings should meet on the same person. What a picture of depravity! It is the persons Christ blesses whom the world curses. (Arthur W. Pink, *An Exposition of the Sermon on the Mount* [Grand Rapids: Baker], p. 39.)

Godly living provokes ungodly men to be resentful. It is the enmity of the serpent against the holy seed. The first standards Christ ever set were so high that the Jews must have fallen over flat on their backs. And then He added to the standards, "And by the way, if you want to live this way, you will be persecuted and chased out of your jobs, your homes, your society. People will speak violently and viciously against you, and say things about you that aren't true."

Why does it have to be like this if we live God's way in this world? Think about why they persecute us. They really don't hate us. Surprised? Well, that's comforting, isn't it? Whom do they hate? Christ. It really isn't us they resent; it's the lives we live—or rather, that Christ lives in us.

In John 15-16 Jesus said to His disciples, in essence, that "if they killed Me, they'll kill you. And if they hate Me, they'll hate you. And if they persecuted Me, they'll persecute you as long as they know that you belong to Me." Jesus revealed holiness in action to an unholy world. The world went a long time and never saw a perfect man. The longer it went, the more smug it became in its contented sinfulness.

When Jesus came, the world saw a perfect Man, and that blew away its self-confidence. It destroyed the basis on which the world had stood. The people of the world felt rebuked, so they killed that perfect Man. They tried to wipe out the standard they could not meet. That's the way it will always be. As long as you and I allow Christ to live through us, we will set a standard that the world cannot attain, and worldly people will desire to remove it so that they can remain in the contentedness of their delusion.

A Christian of ancient time, Aristides the Just, was banished from Athens. He was voted out by the citizens. One said he voted against such a good man "because I was tired of hearing him always called 'the Just.' "(William Barclay, *The Gospel of John* [Philadelphia: Westminster], 2:216.)

It happened to the disciples, just as Jesus said it would. Andrew persisted in preaching and was ordered crucified. According to tradition, he was fastened with cords to a cross, so that death might be slow.

According to tradition, Peter, after nine months in prison, was crucified head down.

Paul was beheaded by Nero.

James, Matthew, Matthias, Bartholomew, and Thomas suffered martyrdom, as did perhaps every disciple but John, who died in lonely exile on the Isle of Patmos.

In Italy in the fifteenth century, a man named Savanarola was one of the greatest reformers and preachers the world had ever known. His denunciation of the sins of the people and the corruption of the Roman Catholic Church of that time prepared the way for the Reformation.

His preaching was a voice of thunder, and his denunciation of sin was so terrible that the people who listened to him went about the streets half-dazed, bewildered, and speechless. His congregations were so often in tears that the whole building resounded with the sobs and their weeping.

The people couldn't handle that kind of preaching, so instead of repenting they burned him at the stake. I really believe that if Christians in our culture were more confrontive about what they believe, and if they really lived the fullness of the Beatitudes, they would find more hostility.

In Don Richardson's *Lords of the Earth* he tells the story of Stan Dale who ministered to the Yali tribe in Irian Jaya, Indonesia. Stan was way up in the Snow Mountains, very high and precarious in a village encamped on the slopes. The Heluk, a thunderous, rapid river, crashes down through the mountains and into the valley below.

The Yali were steeped in an incredible religion. They had little sacred pieces of ground, and they believed that if even a child happened to crawl onto one of them, the child was desecrated and the whole village could be cursed. So, they would throw the child off a cliff into the rapids. If anyone ever said a word against the religious system, he was slaughtered on the spot. So, there could be no rebellion, no change, no possibility of altering anything.

One tribesman tried to point out some of the things that seemed foolish to him. They shot him so full of arrows that he looked like a reed swamp. It was hopeless until a little, undaunted, bandy-legged Australian, Stan Dale, tramped into the village. In an incredible way, that amazing man opened his heart and the hearts of his wife and five children to those savage people who were not only headhunters, but also cannibals.

He came to save them from the impenetrable darkness and death of the terrible beliefs and practices in their culture. What happened to him? I'll quote it directly from the book:

> A priest of *Kembu* named Bereway slipped around behind Stan and—at point blank range—shot an arrow in under his upraised right arm. Another priest, Bunu, shot a bamboo-bladed shaft into Stan's back, just below his right shoulder.
>
> . . . As the arrows entered his flesh, Stan pulled them

out, one by one, broke them and cast them away. Dozens of them were coming at him from all directions. He kept pulling them out, breaking them and dropping them at his feet until he could not keep ahead of them. Nalimo reached the scene after some 30 arrows had found their mark in Stan's body.

How can he stand there so long? Nalimo gasped. *Why doesn't he fall? Any one of us would have fallen long ago!* A different kind of shaft pierced Nalimo's own flesh—fear! *Perhaps he is immortal!* Nalimo's normally impassive face melted with sudden emotion. . . .

Stan faced his enemies, steady and unwavering except for the jolt of each new strike. . . .

Fifty arrows—sixty! Red ribbons of blood trailed from the many wounds, but still Stan stood his ground. Nalimo saw that he was not alone in his fear. The attack had begun with hilarity, but now the warriors shot their arrows with desperation bordering on panic because Stan refused to fall. *Perhaps Kusaho was right!* Perhaps they were committing a monstrous crime against the supernatural world instead of defending it, as they intended.

"Fall!" they screamed at Stan. "Die!" It was a plea—*please* die!

Yemu did not hear Phil [Masters, a fellow missionary] say anything to the warriors as they aimed their arrows at him. Phil made no attempt to flee or struggle. He had faced danger many times but never certain death. But Stan had shown him how to face it, if he needed an example. That example could hardly have been followed with greater courage.

Once again, it was Bereway who shot the first arrow. And it took almost as many arrows to down Phil as it had Stan.

Yemu and the three Danis waited until they knew Phil was too badly wounded to survive. . . .

At the site of the killings, after both missionaries had fallen on the stony beach, the Yali dragged their battered bodies away from the stones and placed each of them in separate forest alcoves, overhung with boughs. . . .

. . . Bunu, moved by fear, beheaded both Stan and Phil.*

There is a price to pay, isn't there? The wonderful end of the story is that the Yali village and that whole territory has now come to know of Jesus Christ, and they do not gather to eat missionaries anymore. They gather around the Lord's table. One of the most wonderful things about this story is that Stan's fifth child, who was a baby when Stan died, was saved by reading the book about his father.

If we confront the world, there is a price to pay. Savanarola paid it. Stan Dale paid it. It will be paid in the future, because in Revelation 9 a group of people under the altar cry out, people who were slain, martyred for the cause of Christ. It will always be this way.

There is always a price for living a kingdom life, but the fruit of it is forever. When we give up this life, we inherit (verse 10) the kingdom of heaven. Though they may take away everything we possess in this world, they shall never be able to touch anything He has given us in the next.

This is the Beatitude that sums it up, and we have hardly started. Promise, posture, and verse 12 are still to come.

*From pp. 304-7 of *Lords of the Earth* (Regal Book), by Don Richardson. © Copyright 1977 Gospel Light Publications, Glendale, Calif. 91209. Used by permission.

11
"Happy Are the Harassed. . ."
—Part two

Matthew 5:10-12

Let's look again at Matthew 5:10-12 and continue the three points that we introduced in the last chapter: the persecution, the promise, and the posture. We began covering persecution, which appears in verses 10 and 11, discussing also the fact that in America we hardly know what the word means.

However, we are on the threshold of some days unlike any we have seen in America. We have been lollygagging around in the aftermath of the Second Great Awakening era, living off the revivals of the past and the benefits of their heritage, but that is fast coming to an end. Not only is government acting against religion, but religion is also acting against itself by proliferating all the cults, isms, schisms, frauds, and phonies.

The government is cracking down on religious groups, and we're seeing the IRS and other agencies begin to push for laws that will have a direct impact on the church of Jesus Christ. Things we once held sacred, even the whole idea of the church, are going the way of Mom and homemade apple pie. They are going to come after us, Jesus says. Why? Perhaps the following story from the days of Paul will help us understand where we fit into the scheme of things.

When a Roman general won a great victory, he was given the privilege of parading his victorious army through the streets of the city. They would carry with them the booty, the spoil, the trophies of war. The general demonstrated to everyone the tremendous triumph he had achieved. At the end of the long procession there always came a little group of captives, tokens of the conquered people. They were men who were now to be led to the arena to fight the beasts and so to die.

Paul says in 1 Corinthians 4:9, "For I think, God has exhibited us apostles last of all, as men condemned to death; because we have become a spectacle to the world, both to angels and to men." Paul saw the apostles as emblems of all truly committed disciples, a group of captives appointed to death.

Moffatt translates it this way: "God means us apostles to come in at the very end, like doomed gladiators in the arena!" The phrase "condemned to death" is a rare term used to refer to criminals paraded as objects of mockery as they were marched to their execution. But then Paul says that we endure anyway, "We are fools for Christ's sake, but you are prudent in Christ; we are weak, but you are strong; you are distinguished, but we are without honor" (v. 10).

He is being very sarcastic there. "To this present hour we are both hungry and thirsty, and are poorly clothed, and are roughly treated, and are homeless; and we toil, working with our own hands; when we are reviled, we bless; when we are persecuted, we endure" (vv. 11-12).

We are not called to ride the white charger into town and be the hot shot. We are not called to be the superstar. We are not called to be the sanctified celebrity. We are called to be appointed to death, and we suffer through this thing. "You look at us as fools," Paul says, "and we are weak and you are strong. You look down on us, you're honorable and we're despised."

How does he react to all that? "When we are reviled," he says in verse 12, "we bless; when we are persecuted, we endure." In verse 13 he goes on to say, "slandered, we try to conciliate; we have become as the scum of the world, the dregs of all things, even until now." The word *scum* simply means *dirt*. In the King James, instead of *dregs* he uses the term *offscouring*, something you scrub off.

You say, "Paul, you're one of the apostles! I mean, we've erected statues of you! We've even got St. Paul's Cathedral!"

Paul says, "We're scum and dregs." The apostles counted the cost. They were willing to pay the price. As far as we know, ten or eleven out of the twelve died as martyrs. I don't know why, but the kind of Christianity we have today isn't that. Can we say in America today that Christians are the scum and the dregs of the world? Why, in some cases we're the stars!

The biggest lights in Las Vegas are for us. We've got our own TV shows. We live in two worlds. We do our thing over here, and then change clothes and do it in church the next night. We dance in Vegas, and then we get up in a Christian meeting and give our testimony. We're the presidents and the congressmen and the famous athletes and the actors and the singers.

Don't misunderstand me. I'm thankful for those who are real believers. I just have to wonder whether or not we've got the picture right. Should it be so easy to be a Christian? Do we waltz the world instead of confronting it? I don't know how this happened. Are we the elite, the acceptable, the rich because we have failed, rather than because we have succeeded?

When Paul came he did not say, "I graduated from the University of Gamaliel, magna cum laude. I'm a world man, I speak many languages, I'm a personal friend of many kings, rulers, famous men. I 'died' once and came back from the dead (Acts 14:19-20). I've ascended into the third heaven (2 Corinthians 12:1-5)." Could he have made it on the circuit today! There is no end to what the guy could have done. Unbelievable testimony. He could have kept you listening for hours.

But what does he say? "Do you want my credentials?" Look at 2 Corinthians 11:23-27. Ladies and gentlemen, I'd like to introduce you to the apostle Paul.

> In far more labors, in far more imprisonments, beaten times without number, often in danger of death. Five times I received from the Jews thirty-nine lashes. Three times I was beaten with rods, once I was stoned, three times I was shipwrecked, a night and a day I have spent in the deep. I have been on frequent journeys, in dangers from rivers, dangers from robbers, dangers from my countrymen, dangers from the Gentiles, dangers in the city, dangers in the wilderness, dangers on the sea, dangers among false brethren; I have been in labor and hardship, through many sleepless nights, in hunger and thirst, often without food, in cold and exposure.

There he is, folks. Second Corinthians 12:5 says, "But on my own behalf I will not boast, except in regard to my weaknesses." I can understand that, can't you? An ex-con, beat up, kicked around, stoned, shipwrecked, abused. Verse 6 goes on, "For if I do wish to boast I shall not be foolish, for I shall be speaking the truth; but I refrain from this, so that no one may credit me with more than he sees in me or hears from me."

He's saying, "I don't want to say anything about myself. I don't want to glory. I don't want to give anybody the wrong impression." He even says, "And because of the surpassing greatness of the revelations, for this reason, to keep me from exalting myself, there was given me a thorn in the flesh, a messenger of Satan to buffet me" (v. 7). I don't know what his problem was, but it was something visible and undesirable. Instead of taking it away, God just said, "My grace is sufficient for you. I've got to keep you humble, Paul."

And Paul agrees, "Most gladly, therefore, I will rather

boast about my weaknesses, that the power of Christ may dwell in me. Therefore I am well content with weaknesses, with insults, with distresses, with persecutions, with difficulties, for Christ's sake; for when I am weak, then I am strong" (2 Corinthians 12:9-10).

As long as we think we can make it on our own press clippings, we do not have the power of God. As long as we think that we can cut it on our own, that we're good, that we've been proved, and that we've got the public relations to make it, we are functioning on the wrong principles.

Paul says, "Everything that breaks me, everything that crushes me, everything that humbles me, I'll glory in that, because that's what makes me depend on God and know I have no resource of my own, and that's when God moves through me to confront the world."

We live in a day when Christianity, like never before, is engaged in an act of self-glorification that must be repulsive to God. We are manufacturing celebrities as fast as than the world is. When our Lord said in Acts 1:8, "You shall be My witnesses," He said, "you shall be my *marturas*." My what? My *martyrs*. There is a price to pay. Who is the Beatitude directed to? Anybody who is a kingdom child.

The crux of the matter is this: the world just does not know God. John 15:21-24 quotes Jesus, "But all these things they will do to you for My name's sake, because they do not know the One who sent Me. If I had not come and spoken to them, they would not have sin, but now they have no excuse for their sin. He who hates Me hates My Father also. If I had not done among them the works which no one else did, they would not have sin; but now they have both seen and hated Me and My Father as well."

Jesus came into the world and exposed the people's sin. They were confronted with the reality of it. If Jesus hadn't come, they could have glossed it over. They were doing a great job at salving their consciences. Their religion had literally closed their eyes to the truth, and in their blindness

they were blissfully marching on toward hell. Christ ripped
off the blinds and said, "Look at yourselves!" They saw
their sin, and they hated Him for what He did.

It isn't really us they hate. It's righteousness. It's Christ.
Just live a righteous life, just be salt, and watch what happens. Have you ever put salt in a wound? It stings. Just be
righteous in a corrupt society and watch what reaction it
brings.

Don't bail out. Don't retreat. Don't pack up your tent and
steal away in the night. Don't hide away studying your
Bible until the Rapture. Get out there and be a "martyr".
The coming of Jesus brought not only salvation, but also the
manifestation of hate from those who loved their sins. Even
though there's a price to pay, we can't bail out.

I can see little Stan Dale, the first time he was shot at, just
prior to the fatal attack. They were all gathered with their
bows and arrows on top of the hill, and he must have said,
"I'm going up there and tell them that they can't do that."
He walked right up that hill. They shot at him. The arrows
were missing, and he just kept right on walking. There's
something exciting about that! He was going to be salt and
light no matter what! It took more than sixty arrows before
he even fell over.

Colossians 1:24 says, "Now I rejoice in my sufferings for
your sake, and in my flesh I do my share on behalf of His
body (which is the church) in filling up that which is lacking
in Christ's afflictions." Paul is saying, "Every time somebody beats me up, they're really getting after Christ." Stan
Dale could have said the same thing, "Every one of those
Yali who shoots an arrow is really shooting at Jesus Christ. It
isn't me they resent; it's the truth I represent." It's Christ the
world is after. It is He the world is still trying to kill, and
they will shoot at whoever stands in His place and speaks
the same truth.

I'm not one trying to make enemies. But I believe in saying what's right—saying it when it ought to be said, where

it ought to be said, to whom it ought to be said—and not worrying about the consequences. For His sake. I hear the apostle Paul, "That I may know Him, and . . . the fellowship of His sufferings" (Philippians 3:10).

We should not seek martyrdom. That's bizarre. But we do not run from it either. And when we get into the middle of it, we do not compromise. Then persecution is followed by a promise.

Promise

What is the promise? "Blessed are those who have been persecuted for the sake of righteousness, for theirs is the kingdom of heaven." Paul, with his mind and his capabilities, would have made it big in this world. Instead, he had absolutely nothing. What did he say about all this? "For I consider that the sufferings of this present time are not worthy to be compared with the glory that is to be revealed to us" (Romans 8:18).

Any loss here could never be compared with the gain in God's kingdom. Twice Christ says "blessed." Those who would willingly stand up for Jesus Christ will know the bliss of obedience and the blessedness of being part of God's eternal kingdom.

Joseph was persecuted by his brothers for righteousness' sake. He ended up in a dry well in the desert, despised and hated. Yet God picked him up and made him prime minister of Egypt.

Daniel, for righteousness' sake, was in the lions' den, about to be lunch for a bunch of hungry animals. But God locked the mouths of those lions and raised him up to be the prime minister of Babylon.

Jeremiah was thrown into a slimy dungeon because of his righteous life. Yet God lifted him up and made his name, as a prophet, as honorable as any one's who ever lived.

If we are willing to pay the price now, God says the glory that shall be revealed is incomparable. Double-blessed are the persecuted, for theirs is the kingdom, and all that the kingdom could possibly contain. I think Christ is talking about the here and now when the living King dwells within us and reveals and gives us the fullness of kingdom life spiritually.

He is also talking about a millennial element when the physical fulfillment of kingdom life will belong to us in that wonderful, renewed earth. I also think He's talking about the eternal kingdom, when we're face to face with the Son of God in glory. He is saying all that the kingdom can possibly convey, all that there possibly can be of God's great and glorious gift, which will compensate for our struggle.

In Mark 10:28 Peter said, "Behold we have left everything and followed You." He was saying, "We've done it, Lord. We've stripped ourselves naked. We've just come after You. We're like beggars in the world."

Christ answered Peter and the disciples, "There is no one who has left a house or brothers or sisters or mother or father or children or farms, for My sake and for the gospel's sake, but that he shall receive a hundred times as much now in the present age." That's the present fulfillment. "Houses and brothers and sisters and mothers and children and farms . . . and in the world to come, eternal life" (vv. 29-30).

See? Here and now. Then and There. It's all ours. What a fulfillment. We are so shortsighted. We want to protect the moment rather than give the moment to God and secure an eternal weight of glory.

The kingdom is the gift of the Beatitude. Did you notice the promise of the first Beatitude was the kingdom of heaven and the last Beatitude ends with the same promise? What this really says to us is that the major promise of the Beatitudes is that you become a kingdom citizen now and forever, and the features in between are elements of kingdom life. No matter what the world does, it can never affect your possession of Christ's kingdom.

The persecution will be there, but when it's endured willingly, the promise is ours. Right now I don't have all the houses and land the Bible talks about. That's going to be in the Millennium and in the eternal state, but there is a sense in which I do own them now, because some of my brothers and sisters and mothers and fathers in Christ have nicer houses than I, and I am invited to enjoy them now and then. That's what it means for the here and now. We all share.

You may give up somebody, maybe even your whole family, to come to Christ. They may isolate you. But look around in your church. There's your family. You may have no place to stay because you've been thrown out of your home. Look around. There are your fellow believers. They've got homes, and they're yours, too. We don't own anything; we just manage it for God.

So, the persecution brings with it a promise, and that means there ought to be a posture we take in persecution.

Posture

What should be our attitude in all this? Verse 12 says, "Rejoice."

You say, "Rejoice?" Rejoice when they're shooting arrows in you? Rejoice while your friends are screaming venom at you? Rejoice while they're whispering behind your back? Rejoice while they're undermining you?

Oh, yes! Rejoice, He says. *Cairo* in the Greek means to be really glad. And if that is not enough, He has to add, "Be *exceedingly* glad," which is *agalliasthe* and means to jump and skip and shout for joy. You say, "You've got to be kidding! I'm being persecuted!"

There are two reasons that you ought to be happy about that. Reason number one (v. 12): "Your reward in heaven is great." Heaven is how long? *Forever.* How long is now? A vapor that appears for an instant and then vanishes away (James 4:14). Which are you investing in?

No wonder Jesus says, "Lay up for yourselves treasures in heaven, where neither moth nor rust destroys, and where

thieves do not break in or steal" (Matthew 6:20). We're
going to get crowns in heaven. The Bible promises it. I believe it has to do with our capacity to glorify God forever,
depending on how faithful we have been here. If I'm going
to be there forever and here for only another twenty years or
so, I'm going to invest in forever! I have just a little snatch of
time, and I want to pile all of it I can into God's bank account
so that it will pay eternal dividends—not for me, but so that
I can place them at His blessed feet in praise.

The word *great* in "your reward in heaven is great" means
just what it says. When God says *great*, he means great,
polus, abundant. It is the fullness of reward. People say you
should serve the Lord out of love, not for reward. If I serve
Him out of love, and He chooses to reward me, that is His
pleasure. I am not going to fight it or question its virtue. By
the time I get to heaven, I will not be proud anyway, so I will
take it all and give it right back in humility. We shall all be
perfect then, so we shall be able to handle reward. That is
why the Lord does not give it all to us here; it would surely
corrupt us.

At the end of 2 Timothy, when Paul pens his swan song,
he says, "In the future there is laid up for me the crown of
righteousness, which the Lord, the righteous Judge, will
award to me on that day; and not only to me, but also to all
who have loved His appearing" (4:8). He says, in effect,
"There's nothing wrong with my longing to see that day.
Nothing wrong with my longing to see that crown. I took
the Lord's gift of salvation, and I'm going to take this one
too."

The second reason that you should be glad is because they
persecuted the prophets who were before you. You say, "So
what? How does that relate? I'm supposed to be happy because they had the same problems I've got? Misery loves
company?"

No, the idea is more that the company is pretty classy.
They persecuted the prophets of God, and if they persecute

you, you are in pretty elite circles. Christ is saying, "If you have any doubts about your salvation, if you have any questions about whether or not you're in the kingdom, the persecution from unbelievers in your life will convince you beyond a shadow of a doubt that you belong to God, because they'll be doing to you exactly what they did to God's called prophets."

Fantastic truth. When persecution comes to me, I just say, "Oh, I know I'm your child, Lord, and I know I stand in the ranks of the prophets!" The world doesn't persecute people who are not the prophets of God, who don't speak the message of God.

In Matthew 23, starting with verse 31, Christ said to the Pharisees, "Consequently you bear witness against yourselves, that you are sons of those who murdered the prophets. Fill up then the measure of the guilt of your fathers. You serpents, you brood of vipers, how shall you escape the sentence of hell?" "Go ahead and do it," Jesus says. "Go ahead and kill Me. You're doing no different than your fathers did."

Hebrews 11 carries quite a catalog of fast spiritual company. It says all those saints suffered this and suffered that, and it concludes that the world was not worthy of them. Then, as recorded in Matthew 5, Jesus says to the crowd that day (and to us all down through church history) words to this effect, "If you follow Me and you preach My truth and live My truth and they persecute you, rejoice that you belong to the righteous line that has descended to you from the prophets themselves."

Persecution is a verification that you belong to a righteous line. Here is the believer's security. Here is the climax of the Beatitudes. Jesus offers salvation and tells how to know you have it. It does not come from some theological prescription. It does not come from knowing that you made a decision way back when. Your security comes from knowing that you are living a confrontive life in the midst of an ungodly world and that you are being persecuted for righteousness' sake.

When that comes, not only will you be rewarded in heaven, but you also stand in the line of prophets of God who have received the same reaction through all of history. In Luke 21:12, Jesus says, "But before all these things, they will lay their hands on you and will persecute you, delivering you to the synagogues and prisons, bringing you before kings and governors for My name's sake." But catch verse 13: "It will lead to an opportunity for your testimony."

In other words, the whole matter will become a testimony to you that you belong to God. Isn't that great? The people in the world, apart from those being drawn by God, cannot handle our kind of life. They cannot stomach it. They do not even understand it. Poverty of spirit runs counter to the pride of an unbelieving heart. The repentant, contrite disposition that mourns over sin is never appreciated by the callous, indifferent, unsympathetic world.

The meek and quiet spirit that takes wrong and is not quick to strike back rasps against the proud, militant, resentful spirit characteristic in our world. The craving after deeper spiritual blessing from the Lord is a rebuke to the lust of the flesh, the lust of the eyes, and the pride of life, as is a merciful spirit to the hardness and cruelty of our world. Purity of heart contrasts sharply and painfully with hypocrisy and corruption. A peacemaker cannot be tolerated by a contentious, antagonistic world.

A great tribute was once paid to John Knox, the Scottish preacher: "He feared God so much that he never dared to fear any man." (William Barclay, *The Acts of the Apostles* [Philadelphia: Westminster], p. 38.) Chrysostom, great Christian of ancient times, summoned before the Roman emperor Arcadius and threatened with banishment if he didn't cease to proclaim Jesus, is said to have replied, "Sire, you cannot banish me, for the world is my Father's house."

"Then I'll slay you!" exclaimed the angered ruler.

"Nay, but you cannot, for my life is hid with Christ in God."

"Your treasures will be confiscated!" came the fiery retort.

"Sire, that cannot be. My treasures are in heaven, where none can break through and steal."

"But I will drive you from man, and you will have no friends left!"

"That you cannot do either, for I have a Friend in heaven who has said, 'I will never leave you nor forsake you.' "

Ultimately, he was banished to the edge of Armenia, but he so continued to influence his friends by letters that his enemies determined to banish him farther away. He died on the journey.

What about us? What are our priorities? What do we say to ourselves? What rings true about us in our minds, in our hearts. Do we understand what the Beatitudes are saying? It isn't the rich, it isn't the proud, it isn't the frivolous, the fierce, the full, the cunning, the warlike, or the favorites of the earthly kings that enter the kingdom.

It is the poor, the meek, the sorrowing, the hungry, the sincere, the peacemaking, the persecuted. They enter, and the proof of their citizenship is that they are hated by the world.

Do you belong? Really?

12
A Final Word

The Beatitudes' urgent message about self-examination is also contained in many of the New Testament epistles, including the book of Hebrews, which was written to Jewish Christians. It is filled with warnings to people who know the gospel intellectually, who understand the call of salvation, but never make the commitment. As the writer goes along writing to the believers, every once in a while he stops and says, "Now I know that in this congregation some of you know this is the truth, but you've never made the commitment."

The readers were Jews, intellectually convinced that Jesus was the Messiah, but they would not commit their lives to Him. They would not take that simple act of child-like faith and throw themselves on His grace and mercy. They would not come to Christ. They were afraid they would be ostracized from their community. They were afraid they would be alienated from their families, or that they would have to give up their current life-styles. The price was too high, so they sat on the fence.

Maybe you fit in there somewhere. You know the truth. You know Jesus is the Christ, the Son of the living God. You know the gospel, and you believe it is true. But you resist making the personal commitment to Christ because of the above-mentioned reasons.

If that is the case, then Hebrews speaks directly to you. Let's look at five warning passages.

Warning number one: Hebrews 2:1-4

> We must pay much closer attention to what we have heard, lest we drift away from it. For if the word spoken through angels proved unalterable, and every transgression and disobedience received a just recompense, how shall we escape if we neglect so great a salvation? After it was at the first spoken through the Lord, it was confirmed to us by those who heard, God also bearing witness with them, both by signs and wonders and by various miracles and by gifts of the Holy Spirit according to His own will.

If you know who Christ is, that He is who He says He is, then the writer is saying that you must give earnest heed to what you have heard, lest you drift away from it. Now, what was the word spoken through angels? The Old Testament law. The point is that if the people who lived under the Old Testament law had to answer for every transgression of it, what makes you think you will escape if you neglect such a fantastic reality as Christ's taking your punishment for you? Certain judgment will result.

Warning number two: Hebrews 6:12

> That you may not be sluggish, but imitators of those who through faith and patience inherit the promises.

And what are the promises? Again, the Old Testament version of the gospel. The writer is saying that you should be a teacher of the gospel because you have enough information. But instead of that, somebody needs to teach you the Old Testament laws again. You are primitive, sluggish, lagging behind, when you should be an example. You have been exposed to the gospel and tasted the power of the age to come, but you need to fully partake of it.

The writer was talking to people who may have seen many of the mighty miracles of Jesus, and he was saying, in effect, "If you've had all this revelation and have tasted and heard and seen the power displayed, yet you turn your back on it and fall away, it's now impossible, hopeless. What else can God do? If you don't accept Jesus Christ when you have full light, you'll never accept and receive Him because He can't do any more than give you full illumination."

If you have read this book this far, you have all the light you need, and you will be held responsible for knowing how to commit yourself to Him.

Warning number three: Hebrews 10:26
> For if we go on sinning willfully after receiving the knowledge of the truth, there no longer remains a sacrifice for sins.

This is very nearly self-explanatory. He is hitting the fence sitters again, those people who have heard it all but have not done anything about it. The sin here is the sin of rejection of the gift of salvation and the willful rejection after hearing the truth. Then there is no more sacrifice for sin. He was saying to the Jews, "You can kill all the lambs you want, slaughter all the goats you want, slay all the bullocks and turtledoves you want, but there is no more sacrifice for sin if you reject the Lamb of God that takes away the sin of the world." After Jesus Christ, there is nothing.

Some people say that God will probably be easier on the people who really knew the most and came to church and got the most information and truth. Wrong. He will be harder on those people. The less you know, the better it will be for you in eternity. If, by God's grace, you have been exposed to the fullness of His truth, you are the most responsible of all. Those who violated the law of Moses were put to death. What of those who violate the Christ of God?

If you turn your back on the truth, God says, "Vengeance is mine; I will repay" (Deuteronomy 32:55; Romans 12:19). You may see yourself as one who knows the truth but has not made up his mind yet. God sees it as you trampling under your feet the Son of God.

Warning number four: Hebrews 12:25

> See to it that you do not refuse Him who is speaking. For if those did not escape when they refused him who warned them on earth, much less shall we escape who turn away from Him who warns from heaven.

Pretty strong stuff. Do not refuse God. In verse 29 he follows with the fact that God is a consuming fire. Someday He will shake not only a mountain, as He did when He gave Moses the law at Sinai, but He will also shake the very heavens with His judgment. What a warning!

Warning number five: Hebrews 3:7-11

> Therefore, just as the Holy Spirit says, "Today if you hear His voice, do not harden your hearts as when they provoked Me, as in the day of trial in the wilderness, where your fathers tried Me by testing Me, and saw My works for forty years. Therefore I was angry with this generation, and said, 'They always go astray in their heart; and they did not know My ways'; as I swore in My wrath, 'They shall not enter My rest.' "

God swore that, and every last one in that generation died in the wilderness and did not reach the promised land. Look at your own life to be sure you do not make the same mistake. It is not popular anymore to be a hellfire and damnation preacher, warning people and scaring them concerning the warnings of Almighty God. However, it appears from this passage that many preachers have been remiss by evolving into a totally love-and-mercy-and-grace message. There are dues to pay, judgments to face.

God is ready to lead you into His rest, ready to usher you into His salvation, yet you harden your heart and are caught in the evil act of unbelief. Do not let it happen to you, He says, as it happened to them in the wilderness. In verse 13 He advises, "Encourage one another day after day." That is why I am burdened with this message to say, "Today, today, today is the day."

Do not reject Christ today. If you do, it will be easier to reject Him tomorrow and the day after. You will harden yourself. D. L. Moody once told an audience to go home and think about the message that he preached and to come back the next night ready to receive Christ. That night the Chicago fire broke out and many of those people perished. Moody said, "I'll never tell anyone *tomorrow* again."

God has extended His love to you. He has reached out His mighty arm and is offering rest for you, rest from your self-righteous activity, rest from your fears, your anxieties, your frustrations, the guilt of your sin. Jesus says, "The one who comes to Me I will certainly not cast out" (John 6:37). It says in Revelation 22:17, "Let the one who wishes take the water of life without cost."

You enter by faith, not works, and you live by faith, not works. Don't put it off. Don't neglect so great salvation. Don't say "tomorrow." Don't say, "When I understand more." Do it now. The Word of God is a sword of wrath and it's twoedged nature means you can't escape. The Word of God can penetrate your heart even if you've been religious and have gone to church, sat on the fence, and known of Christ intellectually. The Word of God will diagnose the true condition of your heart. It'll show whether the profession is real or a sham.

This is not an easy message to write, and I'm not trying to destroy anybody's hope. I just want you to know Jesus Christ. I want you to enter God's rest. Until you cast yourself on Jesus Christ on His terms, as outlined completely in the

Beatitudes, you are living in danger of the judgment of God. Come to Him. Appropriate His love. Live the richness of kingdom life—here and now!

And if you are a believer, truly redeemed, may you know the great joy that comes when an examination of your heart reveals Beatitude character as the direction, even if not the perfection, of your life.

Resources

Barclay, William. *The Beatitudes & The Lord's Prayer for Everyman*. New York: Harper & Row, 1968

Boice, James Montgomery. *The Sermon on the Mount*. Grand Rapids: Zondervan, 1972.

Briscoe, Stuart. *Now For Something Totally Different*. Waco, Tex.: Word Books, 1978.

Lawlor, George L. *The Beatitudes are for Today*. Grand Rapids: Baker, 1974.

Lloyd-Jones, D. Martyn. *Studies in the Sermon on the Mount*. Grand Rapids: Eerdmans, 1959.

Pentecost, J. Dwight. *Design for Living*. Chicago: Moody, 1975.

Pink, Arthur W. *An Exposition of the Sermon on the Mount*. Grand Rapids: Baker, 1950.

Sanders, J. Oswald. *For Believers Only*. Minneapolis: Dimension Books, 1976.

Stott, John R. W. *Christian Counter-Culture*. Downers Grove, Ill.: Inter Varsity, 1978.

Watson, Thomas. *The Beatitudes*. Edinburgh: Banner of Truth, 1975.

Wiersbe, Warren W. *Live Like a King*. Chicago: Moody, 1976.

Commentaries

Allen, Willoughby C., *Saint Matthew: A Critical and Exegetical Commentary*. Edinburgh: T. & T. Clark, 1907.

Barclay, William, *The Gospel of Matthew*, Vol. 1, Philadelphia: Westminster, 1956.

Broadus, John A. *Commentary on the Gospel of Matthew*. Valley Forge: Judson, 1886.

Erdman, Charles R. *The Gospel of Matthew: An Exposition*. Philadelphia: Westminster, 1975.

Gaebelein, Arno C. *The Gospel of Matthew: An Exposition*. Neptune, N.J.: Loizeaux Brothers, 1977.

Hendriksen, William. *New Testament Commentary*. Grand Rapids: Baker, 1973.

Hill, David. *The Gospel of Matthew*. The New Century Bible, Greenwood, S.C.: Attic Press, 1972.

Lenski, R.C.H. *The Interpretation of St. Matthew's Gospel*. Minneapolis: Augsburg, 1943.

MacDonald, William. *The Gospel of Matthew*. Kansas City, Kan.: Walterick, 1974.

Plummer, Alfred, *An Exegetical Commentary on the Gospel According to S. Matthew*. Grand Rapids: Eerdmans, 1963.

Tasker, R.V.G. *The Gospel According to St. Matthew*. Grand Rapids: Eerdmans, 1961.